I0796344

LIVE *Fearless*

A CALL TO POWER, PASSION, & PURPOSE

Sadie Robertson Huff

WITH BETH CLARK

FOREWORD BY LOUIE GIGLIO

THOMAS NELSON
Since 1798

TO MY BROTHER JOHN LUKE, who stomps on the face of fear daily through his confident trust in the Lord, which he has found through faith. Thank you for having enough faith to carry both of us and for believing in me in the midst of my battle with fear. Because of the selfless love you showed me, I will never be the same.

TO MY MOM, who answered every panicked phone call, spoke Isaiah 41:10 to me countless times, and took the time to learn the "Do not fear . . ." verses in the Bible in order to speak the truth I needed to hear. The patience you had with me and the courage you showed me when you did things you were afraid of inspired me. You are the picture of fearless.

TO MY PRECIOUS BELLA, my little bean. Thank you for asking me the tough questions. You awakened my heart to the change that needed to happen.

TO TWO-MAMA, who stayed in Los Angeles with me during *Dancing with the Stars* and covered me in protection. You loved and cheered me on through it so well.

TO MRS. LEISA, LINDSEY, AND ASHLYNNE, who have spent hours sharing wisdom and walking out this journey of freedom with me. Thank you for giving me a place to be open and real, and for mentoring me in the most beautiful way. This book would not be complete without the timing of my relationship with you and the love your family has poured on me.

If you fear anything other than God, you're giving it too much power in your life.

—MY MOM

Contents

Foreword

by Louie Giglio

WHETHER SHE'S WRITING A BESTSELLER, launching a blog, walking at New York Fashion Week, appearing on *Dancing with the Stars* or the iconic TV smash *Duck Dynasty,* or speaking to thousands across the nation on tour, Sadie Robertson does everything with maturity, class, and grace. Excellence is her standard, and others are her focus. She's a role model and a real model—and a stunning combination of authenticity and generosity. She grew up in the spotlight, but she shines far beyond the glow of public attention and adoration.

One of the things Shelley and I love and respect about Sadie is that she is real and an original. She's not caught up in pretense, performance, or appearance but is passionate about leveraging her God-given platforms for the fame of Jesus and the freedom of others. A free life is infectious, and I can't think of anyone better equipped than Sadie to help light the "Jesus-freeing" way to a rising generation.

At the core, I think we all want to live for something that will outlast time and earth. Yet so often we are mesmerized by things that are fleeting—popularity, approval, fame, success. As Sadie learned from experience and as she shares in these pages, even a life filled with all these things can be riddled with anxiety, fear, insecurity, loneliness, and a sense of purposelessness. Though there is nothing wrong with success or recognition or acclaim, the problem arises when we bank our security on the opinion of people. People are a shaky foundation for meaning and worth. To live an eternally significant life, we must be anchored on something eternal. We must be anchored on Jesus.

It doesn't take much research or headline scanning to realize that we live in an age of fear. Fear has many cousins and many names: anxiety, dread, loneliness, and panic, to name a few. More people than ever, young people especially, are living in a dark pit of fear and anxiety.

Social media hasn't helped much. At its best, it's a platform to proclaim the life-saving grace and glory of God. At its worst, it's a black mirror that magnifies our insecurities by highlighting the perceived perfections of others.

The result is an emerging generation that is diminished, paralyzed, and unable to step into God's potential for their lives.

As someone who has lived a harrowing season of life

in the grip of anxiety, I know what it's like to wake up with a suffocating cloud of doom and darkness overhead. I know how it feels to walk with the threat of anxiety lurking in the shadows. Yet by the grace of God, I came through that desperate season and here, by the grace of God, I stand.

In *Live Fearless*, Sadie is open about her own road to freedom from comparison, anxiety, fear, and loneliness. But as you'll see, it's never for the sake of bravado or contrived vulnerability. Rather, Sadie leverages her experience for the fame of Christ, boldly proclaiming His truth and His promises to anyone longing for something firm to stand on. She helps us anchor in true purpose by uniting our lives with the One who loves us as we are and has always dreamed of making us more than we can imagine.

As someone passionate about seeing young people live full and free in Christ, I am moved to see God raising up young leaders like Sadie and inspired by watching her boldly say yes to using her platform, success, and failure to lead people to Him.

You don't have to be around Sadie long to know that her smile, laugh, and persona are infectious. But beyond the catwalks, stages, and TV screens, what's truly infectious about Sadie is the unceasing, Spirit-gifted joy she carries. It's obvious that she's been freed, and I hope you're ready for a deep dive into the path to the same freedom.

You may have picked up this book because you want to be more like the joy-engulfed girl on the cover. And you may be disappointed to discover that she's not giving you a step-by-step guide to becoming Sadie Robertson. In these pages, Sadie's giving you something *more*—leading you to Someone far greater. In these pages, Sadie will lead you to your Maker and into intimacy with Him. If you follow her lead, you'll end up treasuring His Word and awakening to a revelation of His purposes for your life.

I'm praying for you as you start the journey to freedom, believing that these pages will lead you down the best path you've ever walked on. Freedom has a Name—Jesus—and I'm confident you'll grow to know Him better with each turn of the page.

I'm so grateful for Sadie Robertson, and I know you will be too. Jump in and glean all you can from this resource. Take advantage of the built-in space to write, reflect, and process. Let the Holy Spirit guide you, and let God illuminate chains that need to be broken in His powerful light.

For His Fame,
Louie Giglio
Pastor of Passion City Church,
founder of Passion Conferences,
author of *Goliath Must Fall*

Introduction

After years of wrestling with being afraid of various things for various reasons, I can now say that I live a fearless life. This doesn't mean I don't still face situations that are scary; it means God has taught me how to stand strong and not let fear take over my life.

I'm so excited about this book because it's all about something that changed my life and can change yours too. I'm not talking about a little bit of improvement. I'm talking about a major transformation—a transformation that means fear, anxiety, worry, and dread will never again keep you from following your heart or doing what you want to do.

This book is about a journey I'm on with God, a journey I hope you'll take too—a way out of fear and all the other negative things that keep faith from working in our lives. It's my story about learning to live fearless, and I'm convinced it can be your story too.

As you go through these pages, you'll have a chance to express yourself and interact with the message of the book in a personal way. You'll see several ways to chronicle your journey out of the fears that are holding you back in life, postponing God's purposes for you, and maybe even derailing your destiny. As you dig deep into God's Word, answer questions, rise to challenges, receive encouragement, pray, and pay attention to what you believe God is teaching you through this book, I truly believe something inside you will change. When God sees you moving toward freedom, He'll do everything He can to help you get there.

These are some features I've put in the book to help you along your journey toward freedom from fear:

HERE'S A QUESTION: One of the best ways we can grow is to respond to the questions people ask us. As I share my personal stories, I'll stop from time to time and ask a question to help you think about what you've just read, what you may be going through while you're reading, or what God is teaching you.

HERE'S A CHALLENGE: I grew up in a house where challenge was a way of life. That's because my dad always wanted my siblings and me to be confident in what we believe. He knows the world can be a rough place and that people who believe the Bible is true and powerful are not always popular. I don't think it matters to him if we're popular or not; what matters is that we know what we believe, that those beliefs are rooted in the Bible, and that we can be strong in our convictions and able to defend them, no matter how hard someone questions us.

I'm grateful for the way my dad has challenged my brothers and sisters and me throughout our lives. The fact that he got in our faces about certain things has been extremely important in the development of my faith. That's why I'm going to challenge you in this book. The challenges may not be easy, but they'll be good for you. Trust me; I've learned this from experience!

Here's your first challenge: before you start reading, get a pen or a highlighter and be prepared to mark everything in the book that encourages you, seems like good advice, builds your faith, or is worth remembering. I recently started highlighting the books I'm reading, and I've found that when I do it, I am much more focused on what they can teach me and I pay better attention to what I'm reading. Give it a try and see if the same thing happens to you.

HERE'S SOME ENCOURAGEMENT: For some people, meeting a challenge is its own reward. If they think they've owned it, they feel great. For others, meeting the challenge is not so enjoyable, and they find it helpful to hear, "Way to go!" or other words of encouragement. The fact is, the journey through fear can be a little scary.

It just works that way sometimes. You're trying to get the fear out of your life, but you're afraid of the process of getting the fear out of your life. When that's happening, a little encouragement can be a big help. So I'll offer as much encouragement as I can as we go along.

HERE'S HOW YOU CAN PRAY: Years ago, you could drive through almost any place in America and see a bumper sticker or a church sign that read, "Prayer Changes Things." Then someone decided to adapt it and say, "Prayer doesn't change things; prayer changes us." You know what? It's all true. It's not either/or. Prayer does change us, but prayer also changes our circumstances because it asks God to get more involved in them. Maybe you pray a lot and you feel confident in prayer. That's great. Whenever you see something in this book that you want to pray about, go for it! If you're new to prayer or not so confident about talking with God, you can pray the prayers I've written. As you become more comfortable, you may want to adjust those prayers or add to them, going into greater detail with God about whatever is on your heart. I'm a big believer in the power of prayer, and I hope you will experience lots of answered prayers as you journey out of fear.

TAKE NOTE: As you make your way through this book, I'll ask some brief questions in the "Here's a Question" sections, but I also want to ask for some deeper reflection. You may not be able to respond fully with a few words or a sentence, so in these cases you could journal your response in several paragraphs. I'll also share with you some Scripture passages that have meant a lot to me or ask you to find some that mean a lot to you. Anytime I'm hoping you will pay special attention to something, that may mean putting down the book and picking up a Bible or a journal—that's what the "Take Note" section is for.

SO-O-O . . . : Here's a quick, behind-the-scenes story about my experience on *Dancing with the Stars.* The people in charge of the show were great, but they didn't hesitate to point out things I needed to change. One of the big ones was my use of the word *so.* I'm from the South, and when I say the word *so,* I can spread it out over three or four syllables. I also say it a lot. The people at *Dancing with the Stars* said to me many times, "Sadie, you've got to stop saying *so* all the time. Just try not to say *so* so much, okay?"

In this book, no one is telling me not to say *so,* so I'm using that word (and dragging out the *O*s) as a way to summarize the most important lessons and action points of every chapter. When you see the heading "So-o-o . . .," you'll know it's my way of saying, "I really hope you'll remember and apply a few key things, so-o-o here they are . . ."

WORK THE WORD: A pastor friend of mine, Rusty Nelson, says, "You've got to work the Word for the Word to work." This means that while God's Word is always able to change our lives, shift our perspectives, and empower us to live in freedom and victory, it won't happen just because we have a Bible on a shelf or even go to church and open the Bible to read along with the preacher. When we "work the Word," we read it, study it, think about it, choose to believe it is true, share it with others, and pray about it, asking God to use its truth to transform the way we think, speak, act, and live. When we don't understand what the Word means, that lack of understanding hinders our ability to activate it. When we do understand it, there's no limit to the ways it can change our lives.

Obviously, one of my hopes for this book is that it will help you live a fearless life, but my greatest hope is that this book will cause God's Word to come alive in you and make you hunger for it so much that you feel you can't live without it. God's Word always works. If you haven't experienced that for yourself, there's no better time than now.

Before I write anything else, I want to share with you the Bible passage that changed everything for me as it led me out of fear into freedom. I hope and pray it will do the same for you. You'll see it a few pages ahead.

This is not a book you just read and then say, "That

was good." This is a book that can revolutionize your life. It can move you beyond the fear that is crippling you and set you free to soar. If you don't activate the words of the book as you read—fully digest them and apply them to your life—I hate to say it, but you won't walk away fearless. If you do, then you will. You have a part to play in leaving fear behind. Just as you have to "work the Word for the Word to work," you'll also need to work this book for the book to work. Are you ready for an amazing journey, one that will lead you to live fearless? Let's go!

Psalm 46

God is our refuge and strength,
an ever-present help in trouble.
Therefore we will not fear, though the earth give way
and the mountains fall into the heart of the sea,
though its waters roar and foam and the mountains quake
with their surging.

There is a river whose streams make glad the city of God,
the holy place where the Most High dwells.
God is within her, she will not fall;
God will help her at break of day.
Nations are in uproar, kingdoms fall;
he lifts his voice, the earth melts.

The LORD Almighty is with us;
the God of Jacob is our fortress.

Come and see what the LORD has done,
the desolations he has brought on the earth.
He makes wars cease
to the ends of the earth.
He breaks the bow and shatters the spear;
he burns the shields with fire.
He says, "Be still, and know that I am God;
I will be exalted among the nations,
I will be exalted in the earth."

The LORD Almighty is with us;
the God of Jacob is our fortress.

1

It's Not that Things Aren't Scary . . .

Each of us must confront our own fears, must come face to face with them. How we handle our fears will determine where we go with the rest of our lives.

Judy Blume

A FEW YEARS AGO, THE IDEA THAT I WOULD write a book on living fearless would have been unthinkable. I could have written a series of encyclopedias about how to live in fear, but I could not have come up with even one sentence about being fearless. I did not know how to live without fear controlling my life—directing my thoughts, influencing my decisions, answering my questions, preventing me from having fun, and keeping my emotions in a continual state of unrest. It caused me to say no to opportunities that could have shaped and changed my life—opportunities I now wish I'd said yes to.

Had anyone asked me, "Who is the most fearful person you know?" I could have answered without thinking about it for even one second. *I* was the most fearful person I knew!

I once met a girl in the audience of one of my speaking events who made the most interesting comment about fear. She said she felt like it was a disease she could never get rid of. For a long time, I felt the same way.

I went through a season in my late teens when the fear became extreme, and that's when I realized things had to change. But I have to admit that for most of my life, I cannot remember *not* being afraid of something. Just like my long brown hair, my hands, or my feet are with me all the time and I cannot get rid of them, fear was always with me too. The thought of being free from fear was as far-fetched to me as being free from an eye or an ear. It was that much a part of who I was. After all, I reasoned, there were a *lot* of scary things in the world. Why wouldn't I be afraid?

Sometimes I look back and ask myself, "Why were you so scared of everything all those years?" (I can answer that now: because I kept feeding my fear instead of starving it.) God has done a complete work in my life, and I know He wants to do the same for you.

OVERCOMING FEAR MEANS SURRENDERING CONTROL

> God has done a complete work in my life, and I know He wants to do the same for you.

Let me take you back to a few experiences that will show you what a fearful person I used to be. As a child and young teenager (and, okay, even older than that), I was *terrified* of storms. I'm not sure why, but thunder, lightning, high winds, tornado warnings—all those things made me shake inside. Looking back now, the fear seems totally unreasonable, and I'm not sure where it came from.

Maybe I was afraid of tornadoes because, unlike other girls my age who watched Nickelodeon or the Disney Channel, for some reason, I watched the Weather Channel—*a lot.* I was remarkably educated about floods, droughts, hurricanes, and blizzards. I knew about people being rescued from their rooftops and losing power for days. I'm aware that most children aren't fascinated by weather events, but I was unusually interested in what can happen in the natural world and how powerful it can be. I just wasn't interested enough to want to live through a tornado. But I did—kind of, or at least from a distance.

I once saw a tornado from my seat in the car while my family drove from our home in Louisiana to a Texas Rangers baseball game. The sheer force of it captured my attention and terrified me. I can still see the image of the funnel cloud in my mind. But I can also see a mental picture of my cousin, Reed, undoubtedly the toughest and least fearful of the Robertson grandchildren, *freaking out* over the tornado. This guy, who was never afraid of anything and always rushing into things that seemed dangerous, started screaming as loud as he could and even threw his phone to the back of the car!

That episode with the tornado stands out as one of the most frightening events of my childhood because it felt so threatening to me, and there was absolutely *nothing* I could do about it. It was completely out of my control! I didn't know then that navigating situations we have no control over is a necessary step toward breaking free from fear. That's one thing about God; He's the one in control, not you or me.

The tornado incident drove home for me the whole idea that I am not in control of *anything*. It was so much bigger, so much more forceful, so much more frightening than any experience I had ever had. After watching it with my family that day, I didn't want to travel anywhere unless I knew what kinds of scary things could happen.

Seriously, before I went on a trip, I researched the most common natural disasters in the state where I was going. It didn't take long for me to learn what was likely to happen in almost every state in America. Want to know where tornadoes strike most often? Just ask me. Interested in the states where wildfires happen most? I can tell you that. Want to know the places most vulnerable to floods or earthquakes? I still remember them. Oh, and as a bonus, if you'd like to know the details of hurricane season, I could probably help you with those too.

Being afraid of tornadoes and natural disasters isn't terribly uncommon, but I took those fears to extremes. You see, it's one thing to be aware of your circumstances. It's another thing to let them consume and control you—and that's what fear does. Plenty of people are scared of big catastrophes, but it isn't always the big, dramatic events (like watching a tornado from the car window) that make us most afraid. We can be just as fearful of ordinary, everyday situations.

Maybe you've heard that a lot of people struggle with the fear of public speaking. That's been true for me. You may have heard me speak in a large arena or on YouTube, where the whole world can watch and think, *No way! She didn't seem nervous at all!* (If you have, thanks for being there!) Let me just say this: I was the person in elementary school who started sweating and breathing fast if the teacher called on me to read aloud in class. I had to learn to face my fears every time I stepped on a stage or in front of a camera.

> The key ingredient to overcoming fear is not just speaking to it; it's speaking to it in Jesus' name.

Though I truly believe I am living fearlessly, I'll confess that sometimes I still get a little nervous when I speak in front of lots of people, but it's excited-nervous instead of scared-nervous. I used to allow nervousness to keep me from wanting to speak. Now I can hardly wait to get in front of the audience, and I just say, "Go away, fear. I'm not listening to you. I've got a job to do! I mean it. Go away! Not today! Good-bye! In the name of Jesus!"

The key ingredient to overcoming fear is not just speaking to it; it's speaking to it in Jesus' name. When I tell fear to go away and leave me alone in the name of Jesus, I say it with lots of force and a little bit of sass. That short speech has become my anthem. I don't care if I sound a little silly saying it. It works!

If you will stand up to fear, give it a little straight talk, and tell it to leave you alone in Jesus' name, that will get you a long way. But beyond that, it's also vital to trust God *while you're still afraid.* You see, often your peace is waiting for you on the other side of trust. I've had a lot of experiences where God met me once I stared down my fear, pushed through it, and did what I needed to do.

When we're afraid, we have a tendency to pray and ask God for peace *before* we'll step out and do what frightens us. But most of the time, we simply need to move forward.

When we're afraid, we have a tendency to pray and ask God for peace *before* we'll step out and do what frightens us. But most of the time, we simply need to move forward. Once we break through the fear, God gives us the most amazing sense of peace—but usually not while we're still deciding whether to conquer it or not.

If you're waiting for a sense of peace to come so you can deal with your fear, you could be waiting a long time. If you will be brave and march straight into that fearful situation, having faith that God will bring you through it, that's probably where you'll find the peace you're looking for.

HERE'S A QUESTION: How many thoughts of fear consume your mind? On a scale of one to ten, with ten being off-the-charts high, how fearful would you say you are?

HERE'S A CHALLENGE: I challenge you to name your fears because the first step to moving beyond fear is to know specifically what you are afraid of. So go ahead—make a list of your fears on paper or in your phone.

HERE'S SOME ENCOURAGEMENT: Once you get to the other side of fear, once you've had that breakthrough you need, you'll look back on the things you were once afraid of and ask yourself, "Why was I so scared of *that*?" Yep, you'll have the ability to laugh at your fears. That's the kind of freedom I believe you can find in this book.

HERE'S HOW YOU CAN PRAY: *Lord, help me identify what I'm afraid of, and show me how You are bigger and greater than that. Give me security and safety through the truth of your Word.*

TAKE NOTE: The Bible has lots of scriptures that include words like "Fear not" or "Don't be afraid" or something similar (depending on which translation you're using). Here are a few of them. Write down some ways these Bible verses can help you gain victory over fear.

- Isaiah 35:4
- John 14:27
- Matthew 6:34
- Philippians 4:6–7

I DON'T EVEN KNOW HOW TO DANCE!

I was hit with a big fear moment when I received the phone call letting me know that *Dancing with the Stars* wanted me to appear on the show. The timing could not have been crazier. In June 2014, I had attended a meeting about being a contestant. They said they would call me in two weeks to let me know if I had been chosen. Two weeks passed, and no one called, so I assumed I would not be part of the cast. Two months passed and August rolled around. They finally called one Friday, but only to say, "We aren't going to have you on the show. We already have a girl your age for this season."

I was sad and disappointed after waiting all summer for their decision, but I accepted it. Two days later, on a Sunday, they called back and said, "We want you after all, but you'll be a week behind everyone else, so we need you in Los Angeles tomorrow."

The fact that I was a week behind all the other

contestants was not a surprise. I had already seen media reports about people chosen for that season of the show, such as Bethany Mota. Here's the thing about Bethany. She had something like five million Instagram followers when *Dancing with the Stars* chose her. When we went to New York for the announcement on *Good Morning America*, her picture was on the huge screen in Times Square. She's a big deal! Another contestant that season was Alfonso Ribeiro. He eventually became my "California Dad," but when I first heard I would be competing against him, I thought, *No pressure, Sadie. He's only been on* The Fresh Prince of Bel-Air *and danced in a commercial with Michael Jackson.*

Before that, the biggest audience I had ever performed for was in my high school gym during basketball playoffs! Of course I was nervous about dancing on television in front of the whole world!

And then there was me, a teenager from West Monroe, Louisiana, who was not happy about missing basketball season. Maybe you understand why I felt out of place with such well-known, accomplished people. Before that, the biggest audience I had ever performed for was in my high school gym during basketball playoffs! Of course I was nervous about dancing on television in front of the whole world!

But still, I was so thankful to have been asked to be on the show. I was truly honored by the invitation. But the thought of leaving home the next day and being a week behind everyone else was overwhelming. So I said what a lot of people might say when they're overwhelmed: "This is such an amazing opportunity! Thank you so much for asking me. But I just don't think I can fly out tomorrow. This is an intense competition, and I don't want to start out a week behind the other competitors."

My response made perfect sense to me. After all, I didn't know anyone on the show; I had never met my dance partner; and three thoughts kept racing through my mind: (1) What would the Christian community in my small Southern town say? (2) I didn't even know how to dance (minor detail, right?), and (3) It was BASKETBALL SEASON! The more I thought about it, I felt rather awkward and not graceful at all. I could dominate a basketball court, but a dance floor? That was a different story.

Once I hung up the phone, I had a meltdown—and it was major. As soon as they asked me to participate, I decided not to do it because I was so afraid. Fear kicked in, and I could feel it physically.

"I don't even know how to dance!" I shrieked to my mom. I meant it. My school didn't offer a dance class or host a prom. I had never danced in my life! Generally speaking, dancing was not something a lot of people around me viewed favorably (I mean, you've seen *Footloose*, right?), so I was also nervous about what people would say or think about me. That's what the fear of man looks like.

Fear gripped me so tightly that I started bawling, saying, "I'm not going to do it! I can't do it! I know I said I wanted to be on the show, but I don't!" It was quite a crisis at the Robertson house!

My mom stayed up with me that entire night, until 4:00 the next morning. I talked. I cried. She listened. This was a lot for her to process too—the whole idea of sending her sixteen-year-old daughter to Hollywood, to be immersed in a world we knew nothing about. Had I been going on a duck hunt, everyone would have felt okay about it, but a dance competition? That was coloring outside the lines.

I want you to know something about my mom. All my life, she has been my go-to person. She is totally chill. About *everything.* The whole world could be on fire, and my mom would be the one saying, "It'll be okay. We can deal with this." And then she'd get busy doing her part to put out the fire. She's one of those people who doesn't have a fear chip in her wiring; she lives at peace. She takes Proverbs 31:25 seriously—and literally: she really does "laugh at the days to come," and she has no fear of the future.

It means so much to me that while fear was never an issue for my mom, and it *was* an issue for me, she never judged or criticized me. She realized that fear was a genuine struggle for me, and she took it seriously. But taking my fear seriously didn't mean my mom was willing to accept it. She never said, "Oh, it's okay that you're afraid" about anything. Instead, she handled it with grace and said things like, "I understand that you're afraid, but that's not truth." She continually prodded me toward truth and freedom from fear. I'll always appreciate that.

Still, the only time I have ever seen my mom wrestle with a tinge of fear was over my invitation to *Dancing with the Stars*. After all, she'd heard stories about what happened to young people in the entertainment industry—stories about things she didn't want to happen to me. For the first time in my life, my mom and I wrestled fear at the same time.

She finally found freedom from fear when a good friend said to her, "Korie, don't be afraid. Sadie has the God of the universe living inside of her! The devil is the one that should be afraid." Amazing advice! She ended up at peace with my being on *Dancing with the Stars* before I did. Looking back now, I realize that seeing her win her battle over fear ultimately gave me strength to win mine too.

The whole world could be on fire, and my mom would be the one saying, "It'll be okay. We can deal with this." And then she'd get busy doing her part to put out the fire. She's one of those people who doesn't have a fear chip in her wiring; she lives at peace.

MY LITTLE SISTER'S BIG QUESTION

The night of the phone call, Mom and I both got a few hours of sleep. When I woke up, I was still as scared as I could be about *Dancing with the Stars,* and I still thought I would say no to them. Still, I knew the experience could be good for me, but I couldn't find a way to slide myself out of the grip of fear.

The first thing I did that day was to take my little sister, Bella, out to lunch. As I talked about all that had happened, she stopped me and looked me right in the eye. "Sadie, can I ask you a question?" she said in her eleven-year-old, matter-of-fact way. "Is this the fear talking, or is this you talking?"

My little sister had a great point: Who *was* talking? Was it the fear or was it me?

Bella could have simply said, "Sadie, this is not you talking. This is fear talking." But she made her point in the form of a question, knowing that having to wrestle with it would be good for me. Of course it was the fear talking. I didn't want to admit it, but what was I going to do? I got busted by an eleven-year-old!

HERE'S A QUESTION: Are you torn right now because you really want to do something but you're afraid? Ask yourself the same question Bella asked me: "[Say your name here], is this fear talking, or is this you talking?"

HERE'S A CHALLENGE: I challenge you to say yes to whatever you are currently saying no to. Don't let fear make you say no when God is leading you to say yes.

HERE'S SOME ENCOURAGEMENT: Bella's question itself is encouragement. If you know fear is talking, go ahead and silence it. You be the one who does the talking!

HERE'S HOW YOU CAN PRAY: *Lord, give me the strength to say yes when You want me to do something. Give me guidance to know what to do next in my life. I surrender my* no *to You and agree with what You want for me. If You're saying yes, I say yes too.*

THE ENCOURAGEMENT I NEEDED

After lunch with Bella, I had made plans to visit my friend Mary Kate. I was running late. In fact, I became so upset on my way to her house that I threw up in the car. Not pretty, I know. But fear is ugly. It not only cripples and paralyzes us and keeps us from doing what our hearts want to do, it can also mess with our stomachs!

I decided to go to Mary Kate's house anyway because she is the kind of friend whose house you can go to when your nose is running, your face is swollen from crying, and you have throw-up on your shirt. (She's now my sister-in-law, and I love that.)

Still, I thought it might be a good idea to try to calm down a little bit first. So I drove around a neighborhood not far from her house. Suddenly, my brother John Luke appeared. He had been at Mary Kate's house because he was dating her at the time, but for some reason, he ended up just where I needed him at just the right moment. He could see I was falling apart, but he had no idea what was wrong. He tried to get me to roll down the car window and talk to him, but I refused. I was so caught up in fear and so upset that I wasn't thinking clearly.

So John Luke jumped on my car. And he would not get off. I drove around that neighborhood for *forty minutes* with my brother on my car. Talk about love! He was not going to let me be alone, and he was not going to let me go—no matter what.

Eventually, I just decided to pull into Mary Kate's driveway and John Luke got off the car, and we went inside Mary Kate's house. Together, he and Mary Kate helped me settle down and began to talk me through the situation. "You can do this, Sadie," they said. "It'll be great."

I wasn't convinced, but they kept encouraging me. That encouragement was even more remarkable because John Luke *really* wanted to be on *Dancing with the Stars* himself. Had they called him instead of me, he would have been on the plane to LA that day without one bit of fear or hesitation. It would have been pure joy and excitement for him.

As much as he wanted to be on the show, when he saw me having such a hard time with it, he never said,

"What's wrong with you? This is the coolest thing ever, and you're saying you don't want to do it?" He never even mentioned his own dream of appearing on the show. He simply listened to me, spoke truth to me, loved me unconditionally, and showed the most beautiful display of selfless generosity I think I've ever seen. That's why I dedicated this book to him.

By the time I left Mary Kate's house, I felt much better. Their affirmation and support had taken me from being almost torn apart by fear to a place of decision. I ultimately decided to go for it and appear on *Dancing with the Stars.*

Even after the show started, with every practice and every performance, I had to face my fear. Sometimes I felt like arrows of fear were flying at me from all different directions (just like in Ephesians 6:16)—fear of not getting my steps right, fear that something awkward might happen with my wardrobe, fear of letting my partner down, fear of so many new experiences in such a short time. Day after day, rehearsal after rehearsal, televised show after televised show, I gradually found myself no longer dodging arrows but surrounded by a shield of faith that knocked them to the ground. I was still aware of them, but much better able to hold up my shield of faith so they would ricochet off of it, powerless.

I'll write more about *Dancing with the Stars* in a later

chapter, but right now I want to make this point: it's not that things aren't scary. They are, and they will continue to be. But each of us has to come to a deep, personal realization that God has already conquered fear—and by the power of His Spirit, we can live completely free from fear. There's so much more to this life, so much we can experience and give to others if we can break free from fear. If we can learn to let God lead us instead of letting fear control us.

> **Sometimes I felt like arrows of fear were flying at me from all different directions (just like in Ephesians 6:16).**

YEP, I DID IT—AND IT TURNED OUT OKAY

You may know the rest of the story. My *Dancing with the Stars* partner, Mark, and I won second place for season nineteen. I ended up meeting the most amazing people, making friends I hope I'll have for life, and having a blast. Being on *Dancing with the Stars* was the biggest thing I'd ever done—and the most fear producing. But it didn't stay that way.

Once I experienced the situation I had been so afraid of and pressed past my fear, being part of the show turned out to be the most amazing thing I'd ever done—and the one that strengthened me more than anything else ever has. God took all kinds of weaknesses in my life at that time—such as not having any idea how to dance and being afraid of the whole Hollywood scene—and turned them into strengths. Best of all, He used that experience to help me learn to live fearless.

Again, it's not that things weren't scary. I don't know many people who *wouldn't* be terrified to be on an internationally televised dance contest when they had never danced even one step. But as always, even though the circumstances were hugely intimidating, God was even bigger; He still is, and He always will be.

For me, the show was about much more than learning to dance on a stage. It was about learning to dance through life unafraid.

So-o-o . . .

* You—yes, *you*—can overcome fear and quit living your life as a fearful person, just as I did. It's not that things aren't going to be scary, but God has given you power over them.

* When you're faced with something you want to do but you find yourself afraid to do it and even saying no to it, ask yourself the same question Bella asked me: "Is this the fear talking, or is this me talking?"
* Fear will hold you back from some of the most awesome experiences life has to offer, but you don't have to let that happen. You can tell it, "Go away. Not today. Good-bye! In the name of Jesus."

Work the Word

Show me the right path, O Lord;
    point out the road for me to follow.
Lead me by your truth and teach me,
    for you are the God who saves me.
All day long I put my hope in you.

Psalm 25:4–5 NLT

The world wants to take you on a journey. It wants to tell you how to live your life, what you should think is important, how you should think about your work, how you should handle relationships, what you should try to achieve . . . The list goes on. And sometimes, that journey looks good. It can be pretty attractive and satisfying for a while.

But it is not the journey that will glorify God. As John Piper says, "God is most glorified in us when we are most satisfied in him."[1] That's a challenge, but it's a challenge with an amazing reward.

Let me encourage you today to let God—not the world or anything the world tries to inspire you to be or do—be the most satisfying thing in your life. Even if He's leading you in a direction you don't really want to be led and even if you're really scared. It's so important to establish a great relationship with Him and a great love for Him. That's the only way to push past the fear and follow Him. He wants your love, He wants your trust, and He wants to take you on an amazing journey through life that will put to shame everything the world could ever offer. Don't be afraid of God's leading in your life. Step out and follow, because He's taking you somewhere awesome.

2

Who, Me? Fearless?

I learned that courage was not the absence of fear, but the triumph over it. . . . The brave man is not he who does not feel afraid, but he who conquers that fear.

Nelson Mandela

RIGHT NOW THIS INCREDIBLY AWKWARD PERson feels very cool. That's because *I got some ink.*

I got a tattoo of the word *fearless* on the inside of my left arm. I understand that tattoos aren't for everyone. For a long time, they weren't for me either. I never thought I would get one. *Never.* When my dad got them, I would groan and say, "No! I *can't stand* tattoos!" But my tattoo has a story I want to share with you.

Even though fear has been an issue for me as far back as I can remember, during my teenage years, my struggle with it became really intense. When I say intense, I mean that every morning when I woke up, I was afraid of something. Every night when I went to bed, I was frightened for some reason. And throughout each day, I was fearful. To say that I lived my whole life in fear is not an exaggeration.

Every morning when I woke up, I was afraid of something. Every night when I went to bed, I was frightened for some reason. And throughout each day, I was fearful. To say that I lived my whole life in fear is not an exaggeration.

I knew in my head that the Bible says many times, "Do not fear." (In fact, I've included a list in the back of the book of some of my favorite "Do not fear" verses for you to read and memorize.) I knew that was great advice—after all, God said it. I wanted so much to live without being afraid, but I simply could not shake it. I often thought, *Who can blame me? There are so many things in the world to be afraid of, right?* I'd bet you can think of a few too.

Once while wanting desperately to obey God's Word and not fear, yet finding myself unable to do it, I even said to God, *You wrote those words a really long time ago, okay? And look at the world now! There's so much scary stuff going on.*

I didn't *really* think God was unaware of this; I was only making excuses for myself. And I learned that while we are making excuses to God, He has already heard them. He's already considered them, and He still says, "Do not fear." No exceptions. No qualifiers. Just "Do not fear."

NO MORE EXCUSES

You've already heard about one time I said no out of fear: that phone call from *Dancing with the Stars.* Now let me share with you another one. The call came in mid-2015, from the organizer of a ten-day event that would take place in November, called Winter Jam. The yearly Winter Jam events are huge Christian get-togethers for young people, and I was really excited to be asked to participate as a speaker. I was also really scared, so I decided to say no to this opportunity too. (Can you spot the pattern here?)

At that point, my mom must have decided we were *not* going to have another round of drama like we had when I said no to *Dancing with the Stars.* So she nipped it in the bud.

"You're going," she said. "You *are* going to do this."

I heard her, but I was still afraid.

As I thought about that ten-day trip, I kept getting a strange feeling that something bad was going to happen. I thought that feeling was God's attempt to warn me not to go. When I told my mom about it, she said, "God does not produce feelings of fear or anxiety. In fact, it's the opposite. God's Word tells us over and over again not to worry or fear and is very clear that God doesn't give you a spirit of fear, but a Spirit of power. If you're anxious or fearful about this, that is not from Him."

Now, let me say that I do believe God often warns people of danger or even prepares them, but in this case, there was not one bit of danger anywhere around. God was not warning me about anything; the Enemy was trying to keep me from being part of Winter Jam. I should have asked myself Bella's big question again: *Is this the fear talking, or is this me talking?* It was fear. My mom knew it, and that's why she insisted that I go!

When the time came to leave home for the event, my mom practically had to pick me up and put me on the bus! I felt like the new person in high school, so nervous about joining the group. The Winter Jam team included more than a hundred people. Most of them were singers and musicians, some of whom asked me, "Why are you here?"

I wanted to cry! All I could blurt out in response was, "I don't know! I don't have any idea why I'm here!" I didn't want to tell them my mother made me do it.

Before I left for Winter Jam, I was becoming completely disgusted with the way fear was controlling my life. As I started hating the fear that consumed me, I also began to hate the person I was becoming because of it—and that was a major problem.

> More than forty million people in the United States, ages eighteen and older, suffer from anxiety disorders.

About that time, I also saw a statistic that said more than forty million people in the United States, ages eighteen and older, suffer from anxiety disorders.[1] Some people might have said, "It's okay. I'm in good company. Forty million people in the US have varying levels of anxiety like I do." Not me. When I saw that I fell into that statistical group, it made me mad. I didn't want to be a statistic! That's when I knew I really *had* to change. Playtime was over. I *had* to deal with it. No more excuses.

The thought came to me that I wanted more than

just ten nights of giving a message on a platform during Winter Jam. I also wanted to experience God personally during my time on the tour, and I knew that my greatest need was for Him to set me free from fear. So I decided that the start of the trip would be a good time to begin praying and releasing to God the fear that had tormented me for so long.

I began praying intensely—every night—about my struggle with fear, asking God to set me free from its power in my life. It seemed like each night, I gained a little more strength to release a little more fear. As I began to give up the fear to Him, new levels of confidence and courage came to me every single night. It was not a sudden breakthrough, or a realization that I was not as afraid as I used to be. It was something I saturated in ongoing prayer.

As I prayed night after night, the Holy Spirit began to show me that I needed to change the way I was praying. Instead of crying out to God for my situation to change, He led me to cry out for my heart to change. I learned an important lesson through that experience: when we stop praying for God to change our circumstances and start asking Him to change our hearts, that's when we experience the peace that passes understanding (Philippians 4:7).

HERE'S A QUESTION: Are you letting fear run rampant in your life? Have you reached the place where you are ready to deal with it?

HERE'S A CHALLENGE: This is a big challenge, but you can do it. I challenge you to memorize each of these Bible verses. They'll help you a lot on your journey toward living fearless.

- Joshua 1:9
- Isaiah 12:2
- Isaiah 41:13
- Matthew 10:29–31
- Hebrews 13:6

HERE'S SOME ENCOURAGEMENT: Reaching the point where you are totally disgusted with the way fear affects your life can be great motivation to finally deal with it. So my encouragement to you today is to get disgusted with fear if you aren't already!

HERE'S HOW YOU CAN PRAY: *Help me, God, to reach the point that I hate fear and what it does to me—enough to really deal with it. Get me to the place where I want more than anything to be set free.*

TAKE NOTE: Lots of verses in the Bible include instructions from God to specific people, telling them not to fear in certain situations. He said it to Abram (Genesis 15:1), Joshua (Joshua 8:1), Daniel (Daniel 10:12), and Zecharias (Luke 1:13). I encourage you to write a note to yourself using the words "Do not be afraid, [insert your name], as you're facing [describe the situation that is causing fear], because the Lord is with you!" Put that piece of paper where you can see it often, or type the same words into a note on your phone so you can look at them and remember them.

WHERE DID THAT FEAR GO?

Every night, the musicians at Winter Jam played a song called "There Is Power." Every time I heard it, I entered into it completely. I sang it with all my heart. I told God that I believed it. I prayed as I sang, *God, I need the power in the name of Jesus to break this fear off of me.* And I asked God to breathe through me as I spoke to the crowds.

Part of my speaking role each night included participating in a question-and-answer session. For the first seven nights, the founder of the event, Eddie Carswell, sat onstage with me, asking me questions. I would have been over-the-top scared to appear in front of such a large audience by myself, but I could manage the question-and-answer time with Eddie. I wasn't confident; I was a nervous wreck (you know, that old thing about fear of public speaking), but I got through it every night.

On the eighth night, everyone around me was in for a big surprise. The fear that had lived inside of me for so long was gone. God had supernaturally delivered me from it, just as I had prayed He would. I told Eddie I would speak alone that night, that there was something I wanted to say to the audience instead of doing the question-and-answer session.

> **I prayed as I sang,** *God, I need the power in the name of Jesus to break this fear off of me.* **And I asked God to breathe through me as I spoke to the crowds.**

I was praying and praying, getting ready to speak by myself in front of about twenty thousand people, when our security guard walked up to me and said, "Sadie, are you okay with going onstage tonight?"

I said, "Yeah. Why not?"

He then told me about a terror attack that had happened that day at a concert in another country, on a stage very much like this one.

The Enemy is strategic. He is working in many places at once to hurt, kill, and instill fear—and horribly, that day, terror had reared its head in France. Using that massive tragedy and the pain of all those people, he tried to maintain his grip on me. He had held me back and kept me bound in fear for a long time, and he was not going to let me off the hook easily.

Even though I'd just learned about the attack right before going onstage, for the first time *ever,* fear didn't cross my mind. Normally, sadness and fear would have consumed me, and I would have said, "Nope. Not doing it. See ya!" But that night I had thoughts that would have once been totally foreign to me. Thoughts such as: *Yes, I'm going onstage. Tonight of all nights, I need to be onstage. I need to be out there praying for our world.*

I wanted to encourage others to pray too, for the victims and for the state of terror of our world. I wanted to remind them not to give up—to tell them, "This is scary, but if you'll pray for your heart to change, you can face the scariest situations life can offer and still have the peace that passes understanding because you'll know what side of victory you're fighting from."

Several of the artists, musicians, security guards, and crew members on the tour later came to me and told me that seeing my courage that night had a major impact on their lives. They knew that a week earlier, I had been too scared to do the question-and-answers alone. They witnessed the transformation over those eight days firsthand, but they had no idea how intensely I had wrestled with fear before I met them. The people around me actually said to me, "Sadie, you are fearless." I'd never heard anything like that in my life! Fearless? Me? Yes, me.

No matter how afraid you may be right now, you don't have to stay that way. For me, it took becoming totally disgusted with fear to decide that I would no longer let it run rampant through my life.

God did so much in my heart during the ten days of Winter Jam, and I can't begin to write about it all. For now I just want to tell you the most important lessons I learned about dealing with fear. The first lesson is that no matter how afraid you may be right now, you don't have to stay that way. For me, it took becoming totally disgusted with fear to decide that I would no longer let it run rampant through my life. It took the revelation that I did not *have* to live that way. If you're waiting for that same revelation, I just gave it to you! Now you have it too.

Second, if you don't want to stay that way, it's up to you to make a change. No one can deal with your fear except you. And unless you make an intentional choice to confront it, it will keep tormenting you.

Third, once you decide to kick fear out of your life and start your journey toward freedom, the best thing to do is pray. You'll never overcome it on your own; it's too strong. But by God's grace, in the power of the name of Jesus, and with the Holy Spirit's help, you can get fear out of your life and let freedom in.

The more I prayed over my time on the Winter Jam tour, the more I learned to trust God. When I began to trust Him fully with my whole life, that's when the power of fear had to loosen its grip on me. The journey to fearlessness wasn't easy for me, and it may not be easy for you. But I can promise you: it will be worth it.

Sometimes people ask me how they can defeat fear without being a Christian. I don't have an answer for that, because I can only speak about the way freedom came to me—through the Word of God. People can say to me that they don't believe God is real, but no one can ever disprove the freedom I've found through His truth and power.

"FEARLESS"

I went home after the Winter Jam tour and got my tattoo on Thanksgiving Day, saying, "I never want fear to stop me from doing anything else in my life. I never want fear to make me say no again. I never want fear to be even the slightest problem for me. And if I ever have just a tiny fearful thought, I want to be able to say no to it immediately."

So I got the tattoo on the inside of my left arm because that's where I can see it best. It's not for anyone else. It's not to brag or to be cool. It's there so I will have a permanent reminder that God has defeated fear.

I once read a definition of fear that called it *the belief that something bad is going to happen.* As I thought about that, I said to myself, "That's true." And then I realized that *faith* is the belief that something *good* is going to happen (you can read about that in Hebrews 11:1). Faith and fear both involve belief, and they both involve believing things we cannot see. We all have to choose which side to land on, and my tattoo says to me every day, "Sadie, no more thinking something bad is going to happen. You're no longer on the side of fear; you're on the side of faith, and you can spend every day of the rest of your life believing that God has good things in store for you!"

Getting a tattoo itself can be a scary experience. You know, needles on the skin and all. But amazingly, when I got mine, I wasn't the slightest bit afraid. In fact, I was so happy that I could hardly keep from laughing while the tattoo artist was working. If I examine my tattoo closely, I can see a place where he actually messed up while I was shaking with laughter. That doesn't bother me at all, though. I think it's great that my tattoo isn't perfect because I was happy while doing something that could have been frightening.

Here's another thing: when I used to get overwhelmed by fear, sometimes my arms would go numb. I would take one hand and grab the other arm and shake it, trying to get the blood to flow and the numbness to stop. Now if that happens, I can grab my left arm with my right hand and know that I am grabbing hold of fearlessness in the name of Jesus. Pretty cool.

> The tattoo on the inside of my left arm is there so I will have a permanent reminder that God has defeated fear.

You might think that a tattoo would be something like a permanent trophy to commemorate a win in the battle against fear. It's not. It's actually only the beginning of the war. That's because no matter how many victories a person wins over fear, it will challenge us again and again. It's good to celebrate each time we break free from fear, but it's also important to remember that things aren't going to stop being scary. My tattoo is just a message to me and to everyone who sees it that I'm not going to stop being fearless. It declares to me that I am now someone who will always shout yes when fear tells me to say no.

Sometimes being fearless comes easily to me. Increasingly, it's my default position. But I would be fooling myself to say that I am *never* scared of *anything* anymore. Instead, I am learning more and more how to handle the temptation to fear, how to stop it before it takes over my mind, and how to defeat it with God's help one situation at a time.

Fearless is a word that describes who I am today. It also describes who I am continually becoming. I want you to continually become more fearless every day you live. I know it's possible.

A SECOND CHANCE

One of the greatest parts of my Winter Jam experience came after the tour was over, after I'd had my tattoo for a while, and after I'd had some time to really get established in living a fearless life. About a year following the conclusion of the ten-day tour, Eddie invited me be part of Winter Jam 2017, which was not a ten-day event, but a three-and-a-half month, forty-six-city tour!

When I got the invitation, there was no fear in sight. All I felt was pure excitement, total joy, and lots of gratitude for having been asked to participate again.

I said to Eddie, "Thank you so much for asking me to do this again. I gave you no reason to trust me last time you had me on the tour. I wasn't very good on the platform because I was so consumed with fear and anxiety. I didn't bring much to the team or to our times together offstage. I was nervous and I felt awkward almost the whole time. I did not give you or God any reason to believe I could come back and do a better job—so I really, really appreciate that you're giving me a second chance."

This invitation was one of the most beautiful experiences of redemption I had ever encountered.

When I got to the first city and stepped onstage the first night of Winter Jam 2017, I thought, *Wow. Being here shows me that my fear really is gone. What I was so afraid to do a little over a year ago, I am excited to do tonight. Here I am to tell people my age that God can turn their weaknesses into strengths, and it's so much more than words to me. It's not just something I'm going to talk about. It's something I'm living right this minute. I'm living proof that what I'm going to preach tonight is true. One hundred percent. That's so cool.*

So-o-o . . .

* When God says, "Do not fear," He means it. We aren't supposed to fear anything at any time for any reason. And yet, we all do. So how do we obey His "do not fear" instruction? He will help us.
* One of the most important lessons I have ever learned was expressed in the words to the song I heard each night during Winter Jam. There *is* power in the name of Jesus. His name has power to break every type of bondage, and by praying in His name you can gain victory over fear, just like I did.
* Becoming fearless is both an achievement and an ongoing journey. For me, it's also a commitment and a way of life. I pray it will be the same for you.

Work the Word

> Do not fear, for I am with you;
> do not be dismayed, for I am your God.
> I will strengthen you and help you;
> I will uphold you with my righteous right hand.
>
> Isaiah 41:10

If anyone knew how to work the Word with a specific Bible verse, it was my great-grandmother. Even when she was very old and could not remember much, she remembered this verse.

My great-grandmother had a strong Southern accent and kind of a dramatic way of speaking. She believed this verse with all her heart, so when she said it aloud, she said it slowly, with conviction and passion. It's almost like she put an exclamation point after "So do *not* fear!" Then she stretched out the word *I* for two or three beats. Every time she said it, she was emphasizing that *God* is the One who is with us, that *He* is our God, that *He* strengthens us and helps us, and that *He* upholds us with His righteous right hand. We can't do any of these things for ourselves. God does them for us, and we can trust Him to do them every time we need them.

Everyone in our family can quote this verse word for word. We've *got* this one because we heard my great-grandmother say it to us for years. As her health declined and she knew her life was coming to an end, we heard her say it more than ever. I think it was her way of finding comfort in her last days. She was working the Word for all it was worth, speaking it over herself, using it to find strength for her journey to heaven. I believe she knew that.

But what I'm not sure she knew is that every time she said it, she was giving us comfort and strength as well. She was putting the Word to work on those who loved her, and that's the best gift she could have ever given us.

3

The Purpose of Plankton

Mostly I sit at home in the evenings watching the box and hoping one day I'll evolve into plankton.

Tom Holt

IN MY FAMILY, WE GROUP TEXT. OUR GROUP text is named "swag fam." It's great for keeping in touch, especially since so many of us travel frequently.

When I'm having a rough time, I know not to look for sympathy from my dad because he's not the most sensitive person in the world. Once, to "encourage" one of us who was having a bad day, he sent a group text to "swag fam" with a picture of a man in a pretty hilariously bad situation with the comment, "At least you're not that guy." We all thought Dad's response was really funny, so from then on when something bad happened or someone in our family had a high-stress, "the world hates me" kind of day, we began to say, "At least you're not that guy."

A little while later we all were sitting around the living room and started going back and forth trying to come up with the best line about "At least you're not [fill in the blank]." I have to admit that we came up with some pretty funny things. Unfortunately, one of my lines got crickets in response. No one got it. I said, "At least you're not a plankton."

I don't even know where that came from. I didn't even know what plankton was at the time! No one else knew much about plankton either, so maybe that's why they just stared at me in awkward silence before saying, "Wait. *What*?"

Trying to redeem myself and unable to think of anything related to plankton except SpongeBob, I said, "Okay, I don't know where that came from, but it might be brilliant."

I grabbed my phone, Googled "plankton," and told everyone what I learned from Wikipedia: "Plankton . . . are a diverse group of organisms that live in the water column of large bodies of water and that cannot swim against a current. They provide a crucial source of food to many large aquatic organisms, such as fish and whales."[1]

Happy to be able to defend my case, I said to everyone, "Okay, seriously, find me something with a more unfortunate definition, and I will continue to let you take verbal shots at me. But first, please, someone tell me what could be worse than being a plankton! I think there's probably nothing in the universe lower than this stuff! Of all the things you're glad you're not, plankton takes the cake."

> I felt the challenge and sensed that God was trying to teach me something, so I set out on a quest to understand as much as I could about plankton.

So "At least you're not that guy" gave way in our family to "At least you're not a plankton" whenever someone thought they were having a hard time.

And then one day, plankton took on a whole new meaning for me. I felt the Spirit of God breathe a question in my spirit: *"But what if you were? What if you were plankton? Could you find purpose and passion in something I gave life to? Is plankton really the lowest of the low?"*

My first thought was, *What a random question.* But then I felt the challenge and sensed that God was trying to teach me something, so I set out on a quest to understand as much as I could about plankton.

WHAT ARE PLANKTON ANYWAY?

I can't explain plankton the way a scientist could explain it, because, well, I'm not a scientist. But I am a seeker of God's truth, and I love to discover new things that spark my wonder of the Creator we serve. I love that God's truth is all around us and that all we have to do to find it is open our eyes, ask a few questions, and watch for the answers. I found a lot of answers as I learned about plankton—yes, even tiny, insignificant plankton—and I want share them with you.

First, the English word *plankton* comes from the Greek word *planktos,* which means "wanderer." So plankton are wanderers. Hmm . . . kind of like you and me.

I also learned that unlike any other fish in the ocean, some types of plankton swim vertically. This may not seem like a big deal to you until you understand that *swimming vertically enables plankton to provide about 90 percent of the ocean's photosynthesis.*

Let me just pause there for a moment. If you remember photosynthesis as nothing more than a word on a notecard from science class, let me explain. According to photosynthesiseducation.com (yep, there really is a whole website dedicated to photosynthesis education), photosynthesis is the process by which plants make their own food. It provides two important things: food and oxygen. I learned on their site that "while it is important that photosynthesis provides food and oxygen, its impact on our daily lives is far more extensive. *Photosynthesis is so important to life on earth that most living organisms, including humans, cannot survive without it.*"[2]

Did you get that? You and I could not even stay alive without photosynthesis, and a kind of plankton called *phytoplankton* are the key ingredient in most of the ocean's photosynthesis! They are also providing 50 percent of the oxygen you are breathing right now.[3]

How does this happen? During the night, phytoplankton journey toward the surface of the ocean. They receive light there and absorb energy from the sun. Then, during the day, they go back to the bottom of the sea. This is the biggest migration that happens in the world each day.

These plankton are drifting past the most dangerous of their neighbors, risking their lives just to get to the light of the sun. You may be thinking, *Oh, that's neat. They are starving for the light for themselves.* But no. You see, the overwhelming, breathtaking beauty of the purpose of plankton is this: once they receive light from the sun by swimming near the ocean's surface, a safe haven from their enemies, they don't stay there. They swim back down to darkest depths of the ocean—to the most bizarre companions—fueled with light. That's how they fulfill their great and glorious purpose, which is to provide energy, oxygen, and life through the power of the light they share—light they first had to receive themselves.

So what's my point? The world of the sea is so extraordinary and so complex, but God is so detailed and so amazing that even tiny, microscopic organisms have a purpose in His plan. They are little, usually invisible to the human eye, but their purpose is huge. If God can breathe purpose into the life of plankton, just imagine what He can do through you.

> If God can breathe purpose into the life of plankton, just imagine what He can do through you.

About the same time I was learning about plankton, Isaiah 26:7–8 came to my attention. When it first came alive to me, it was not from any one Bible translation, but a paraphrase from Passion City Church: "Yes, Lord. Walking in the way of your truth we eagerly wait for you, for your name and your renown are the desire of our souls." Since my mind was on the watery world of plankton, I began to envision them down in the darkness of the ocean, waiting and yearning for the light so they could fulfill their purpose. So I'm thinking about these little microscopic organisms that provide food for bigger fish, which in turn produces energy for most of the life in the ocean and oxygen for half the world or more, and I'm saying, "Well, you know what? Maybe my spirit needs to learn a lesson from plankton." The way they eagerly wait for the light and then take it back to the darkness is exactly what I want my life to reflect.

TAKE NOTE: Sometimes we try to swim with the flow of our own current, running after the things in front of us. Maybe it is time to stop, look up, seek, wonder, and follow God's lead. Let go of the reins on your own life and drift into His presence.

With words, a drawing, or some other creative expression, describe what it would be like in your life to stop, look up, seek, wonder, and follow God's lead as you release the rein on your own life and drift into His presence.

THE BIGGEST MIGRATION IN THE WORLD

As I wrote earlier, plankton move in the biggest migration that happens on earth every day. But priest and theology professor Daniel Groody points out a migration of a larger kind: "The greatest migration story of all is the story of God migrating to humans in the person of Jesus so that one day we may all migrate back to God."[4]

I've mentioned the word *migrate* a couple of times so far in this chapter, and I want to make sure to define it. To migrate simply means to change or to move from one place to another. In this sense, you're migrating too. And along the path to our all-important migration toward God, we will all undergo smaller migrations, or changes, in life. For instance, most people reading this book, maybe even you, are probably about college age or in high school thinking about college someday. That is a migration of sorts. At some point, you'll be leaving home, starting a new journey.

A migration like this is not without its scary moments. I was thinking about my own journey recently and checked the Internet to see what the biggest fears of college students are. I came across some information on GrowingLeaders.com that really alarmed me.

> Students are scared they are going to sacrifice their beliefs because the odds of staying true to their convictions are against them.

In an informal survey of students a few years back, Growing Leaders founder Tim Elmore shares that students are fearful of the direction the United States is heading. They see what has happened to our country over the years, and they are afraid of living in it in the future.

Another big fear was shocking to me: students are scared they are going to sacrifice their beliefs because the odds of staying true to their convictions are against them. They want to live according to their values, "but life has been very convenient for them, with little need to sacrifice for what is right, and they're not sure they can do it."[5]

The scariest thing here is the thought that many of us college-age Christians might be willing to sacrifice a relationship we have worked our whole lives for, just to save our reputation and fit in with the world.

So many of us have had so few real challenges in life—the kind that blossom into a confident trust in the Lord when we are thrown into the world. The character of God covers this fear, but we have to *know* His character in order to *see* His character in the midst of our fears.

I'm talking about *big* fears here. Not just fears such as "I'm afraid I won't know how to do my laundry and my red shirt will fade all over my white shorts" or "I'm afraid I might not get along with my roommate." According to Tim Elmore's findings, students' fears are serious; they are fears about the fate of our nation, our world, and our souls.

Apparently we are afraid we are going to sell out an extraordinary relationship we have had all of our lives—a relationship with God—to achieve a very average reputation. If we really believed in the truth of God and His power, we wouldn't have these fears.

One way to face fear as we start any migration is to change our posture as we walk into the world. Many of us are acting like following God means we live a life of misery and saying no to all of the "fun" things in life. Perhaps we haven't yet realized that following Christ is the way to an abundant life—it's the way to true joy and a great adventure! If we walk around acting as though living in a relationship with Jesus is boring and miserable, no one will want to join the migration to Him. But if we go to the world as the salt and light, as Jesus calls us to, with celebration of what He has done in our lives, others will want to be a part of it too.

One way to face fear as we start any migration is to change our posture as we walk into the world. If we go to the world with light and celebration, they will want to be part of it too.

To believe and live by God's truth and His promises, we have to be like plankton. We have to get to God often and feed ourselves on His Word and His presence. We're not going to provide energy for ourselves, much less for others, by just going to the top one time and then spending the rest of the time swimming around in the darkness. It's not like we can say, "I went to a great Christian conference" or "I had a great worship experience in church today, so I've checked that off my list." No, it means going back to the top—back to a very personal place with God—every single day.

I don't want to give the impression that a vibrant life with God means nothing will ever go wrong or that every day will be a party. That's just not true. Life does have its challenges and disappointments. Sometimes it gets really, *really* hard or sad. Would you be surprised to know that plankton can teach us a lesson about those difficult times too?

You see, plankton occasionally find themselves on the seashore, right there on the sand with the shells and sandpipers. You might be surprised to learn that a jellyfish is a type of plankton, and maybe you've seen jellyfish on the beach.

If you're on a beach and you step on a certain type of bioluminescent plankton, it glows. Yep, it will just light up right there on the sand. If you step on something that doesn't glow, it's probably not in the plankton family. (I strongly encourage you not to step on a jellyfish, though. That could really hurt).

Get this: in order for the plankton to glow, it has to be stepped on. It only gives off its light when pressure is applied to it. Hmm. Sort of like what God does in your life and mine. The pressures we face are not intended to hurt us or discourage us. They are designed to bring out of us the light that is in us because of our love for God and our relationship with Him. When the light comes out of us, it changes the world.

HERE'S A QUESTION: What if you spent the next three months going to the top and receiving the light? Not just today, not just this once, but for about ninety days in a row, in daily prayer and Bible reading.

HERE'S A CHALLENGE: You probably know how I'm going to challenge you: Just do it. Spend the next three months going to the top and receiving light, then sharing it with others. It's not quite as simple as it sounds. The process of getting light may seem easy, but it's not—because it requires you to expose your darkness. In receiving light and sharing it with others, you'll have to get rid of any darkness inside of you. When I first started receiving light from God and learning to share it, I had to do a couple of things that were not easy: (1) I had to stop some of my social media activities, and (2) I had to wake up an hour earlier than I wanted to each day in order to pray and spend time in God's Word. This challenge truly changed my life.

HERE'S SOME ENCOURAGEMENT: All I can say about ninety days of getting light from the top and using it to help others is that I think it would revolutionize your life. If you'll give it a try, you just might find that it changes everything for you.

HERE'S HOW YOU CAN PRAY: *Lord Jesus, I am in awe and wonder of who You are. I want to know more about You. I want to see more sides of You. Enlighten my mind to see a new side of Your holiness today. As I seek Your face, fuel my heart with passion and give me the strength to bypass my enemies to fulfill the purpose You have given me. Thank You, God, for bringing meaning to my life.*

FROM THE DEEP WATERS

One of my favorite people in the Bible is David. I think he was actually *convinced* that God was with him. That's huge. Did it keep David from making mistakes? Nope. Despite David's sins, he was called a man after God's own heart (Acts 13:22). And I think he was one of the most willing people in the whole Bible—willing to follow God, to worship with all his heart, to lead a nation, to humbly repent when he sinned, to receive God's forgiveness and go on. He was willing in so many ways.

When Samuel the prophet went to the town of Bethlehem to anoint David as the future king of Israel, he didn't know yet exactly who would be king. So he went to the home of Jesse because God told him that He had chosen one of Jesse's sons for the job (1 Samuel 16:1). When Samuel asked Jesse to let him see his sons, Jesse did everything he could do to avoid mentioning David. David was just the shepherd boy, so maybe Jesse thought there was no way he could ever be king.

Pause right here and think about this: before David was King David, before he was warrior David, before he was champion David, before he was musician and psalmist David, he was shepherd-boy David. Before that, he was David, son of Jesse, living in Bethlehem. All his life, from its very ordinary beginnings, David let God lead, and he walked forward with no agenda. That's why God was able to do through him what only God can do.

Life wasn't always easy for David. I'll write about his encounter with the giant, Goliath, in another chapter, but here let me just say that he had to fight a lot of enemies. He did this, of course, as Israel's king, but he also did it on a personal level when Saul (the previous king) wanted to kill him (1 Samuel 19). In 2 Samuel 22, toward the end of David's life, he wrote a song to the Lord as he remembered how God delivered him from "all his enemies and from the hand of Saul" (v. 1). He said, "The Lord is my rock, my fortress and my deliverer; my God is my rock, in whom I take refuge, my shield and the horn of my salvation" (vv. 2–3). See how personal these words are? They are the words of someone who *really* knows God and has a deep, personal relationship with Him.

Later in this chapter, David writes, "He reached down from on high and took hold of me; he drew me out of deep waters" (v. 17). You know what that tells us, in the context of the rest of his story? Two things: (1) David could depend on God to deliver him because he was coming from a place of already being delivered. The reason he had already been delivered was that he had already fallen in love with who God is. When he cried to God, it was in the context of a relationship, not merely to save his life. And (2) you can take this as a promise: God will pull you from the depths of the ocean, whatever your ocean is. If it's feeling left out, not knowing what your future will bring, struggling with some kind of temptation, or something else, God is able to reach down and bring you out. He will bring you back to the top—just like plankton.

God was able to do through David what *only* God can do.

TAKE NOTE: Have you ever felt like you were in deep waters and you needed God to reach down and rescue you? How would you describe that feeling? How can Isaiah 43:2–4 encourage you? It says,

> "When you pass through the waters,
> I will be with you;
> and when you pass through the rivers,
> they will not sweep over you.
> When you walk through the fire,
> you will not be burned;
> the flames will not set you ablaze.
> For I am the LORD your God,
> the Holy One of Israel, your Savior. . . .
> You are precious and honored in my sight."

WHICH BRINGS ME BACK TO THE QUESTION . . .

So what if we are plankton? What I once thought was the lowest of the low, I now know is keeping all of us alive! Now that I think about it, I *want* to be plankton! I want to swim up to the light and bring it back to this dark world. I want to provide light and energy and life to those around me.

Remember the meaning of *plankton*? It comes from a word that means "wanderer." We are all wanderers in some way. We all drift around in life a bit searching for our purpose. God created us with the ability to question and doubt. He gave us the desire to have a meaningful life, to make a difference. Maybe you can look back over the generations of your family and see that the wandering has brought you here. To you. To now. It may take generations before it is seen. But I know this: if we keep swimming vertically, if we keep going to the top, if we understand that in our brokenness God's light can shine the brightest, then wherever we find ourselves—if we are "that guy" or worse, a plankton—we can live passionately with purpose.

Let me encourage you not to get lost swimming around aimlessly or left at the bottom of your ocean in the darkness. Go to the top. Receive the light of God

We are all wanderers in some way. We all drift around in life a bit searching for our purpose. God created us with the ability to question and doubt. He gave us the desire to have a meaningful life, to make a difference.

in your spirit. Soak Him in. Do not let where you came from, how other people may define you, labels people put on you, who your family is, or what has happened in your past determine the path of your future. Instead seek your path through the light of Jesus. Let your passion for Him give you the fuel to press past fear, insecurity, or other negative emotions so you can realize your purpose.

When you are up there basking in the light, what is God fueling in your spirit? What is He moving in your heart? That is what you have to offer the kingdom. That's where little bitty plankton like you and me can provide light and energy and oxygen to the entire world. There are no limits. If we, who live in a world of darkness, could only soak in the light! If a microscopic organism can bring life to 90 percent of the ocean, then I believe that if we are willing to swim up to the light, to receive what God has for us, then we can live out our purpose with passion and truly light up the world.

* Plankton are microscopic, yet they provide oxygen for more than half of the world. Just think about how much bigger-than-microscopic you are and how much good you could give to the world.
* Even the smallest microorganisms have purpose as

God's creatures. Just like plankton, you are created with a purpose. Do everything you can do to fulfill that purpose with passion. If the Lord put purpose in plankton, you'd better believe He put purpose in you!

* Whenever you go through a personal migration, determine to cling to God and not let go of your faith. Every day, keep going to the light and keep sharing it with others.

Work the Word

When the servant of the man of God got up early the next morning and went outside, there were troops, horses, and chariots everywhere. "Oh, sir, what will we do now?" the young man cried to Elisha. "Don't be afraid!" Elisha told him. "For there are more on our side than theirs!" Then Elisha prayed, "O Lord, open his eyes and let him see!" The Lord opened the young man's eyes, and when he looked up, he saw that the hillside around Elisha was filled with horses and chariots of fire.

2 Kings 6:15–17 NLT

This passage is awesome to me because it shows the power of prayer. Elisha's servant was terrified by the soldiers, horses, and chariots he saw. He was in a panic because he thought the king of Aram would harm Elisha. This illustrates a point I have been making throughout this book—it's not that things aren't scary. They are. It's that God has already conquered the fear that tries to consume us. Elisha saw that his servant was frightened, so what did he do? Let me first say what he didn't do. He did not try to reason with the servant or talk him out of being afraid. He didn't resort to natural solutions. He went straight for a spiritual solution—he prayed. After he prayed, the servant was no longer afraid! When God opened his eyes he could see that God had placed horses and chariots all around Elisha, to fight for him and keep him safe.

What a great gift you can give to other people simply by praying for them. When you pray for others, it's so important to be rooted in the Word so you can pray God's Word over them, using the words of Scripture in your prayers. If people in your life are afraid, you can be the one who is fearless, like Elisha, and say, with the words of this verse, "God, open their eyes and let them see. Let them see this situation from Your perspective. Let them see themselves the way You see them. Open their eyes, God, and show them what they need to see so they won't be frightened anymore."

4

Jump Off the Crazy Train

Fears are nothing more than a state of mind.

Napoleon Hill

IF YOU'VE READ MY BOOK *LIVE ORIGINAL* OR heard me speak somewhere, you may know about my Two-Mama. She's my mom's mom, and she has all kinds of wise little quotes and sayings. One of them is: "Quit camping out in your mind." Camping out in your mind simply means focusing on a certain thought, usually a negative one, and staying there—like you pitch tents in a campsite. That indicates you aren't leaving anytime soon. You intend to stay a while and soak up the experience. Camping out around the wrong thoughts never turns out well, and it can lead to real trouble.

When a scary thought first works its way into your brain, you have a choice. You can camp out on that thought in your mind, like my Two-Mama says *not* to do. Or you can deal with it right away to keep it from becoming bigger and scarier than it already is.

I'll guarantee you, if you camp out on a fearful thought long enough, the next thing you know you'll have another fearful thought, then another, then another. And before you know it, you'll have a first-class ticket on the crazy train. I'm going to tell you what the crazy train is later in this chapter, but to help set it up, I first want to mention something that makes the crazy train possible. It's an old acronym for fear: False Evidence Appearing Real. You can read about it in the next section.

When a scary thought first works its way into your brain, you have a choice. You can camp out on that thought in your mind, or you can deal with it right away to keep it from becoming bigger and scarier than it already is.

HERE'S A QUESTION: How do you respond physically to fear? Wouldn't it be nice if that didn't happen anymore?

HERE'S A CHALLENGE: Probably the very best Bible verse there is about the mind is Philippians 4:8: "Fix your thoughts on what is true, and honorable, and right, and pure, and lovely, and admirable. Think about things that are excellent and worthy of praise" (NLT). My challenge to you right now is to memorize this verse. Then whenever you have a fearful thought, remember these words and ask yourself, "Does this thought fall into one of these categories?" If the answer is no, stop thinking it and think about something that does.

HERE'S SOME ENCOURAGEMENT: You don't have to be afraid. You can stop fear where it starts—in your mind.

HERE'S HOW YOU CAN PRAY: *God, help me to take captive every thought in my mind that is not of You and silence the whispers of the Enemy in my ears. I choose to fill my mind with thoughts that are pleasing to You.*

TAKE NOTE: Here's an exercise that I think will be really helpful for you as you learn to replace fearful thoughts with better ones. Use a dictionary or a dictionary app or website on your phone and look up what each of these words from Philippians 4:8 means. The better you understand what the words mean, the better you'll be able to think these kinds of thoughts.

- True
- Honorable
- Right
- Pure
- Lovely
- Admirable
- Excellent
- Worthy of praise (look up *worthy* and *praise*)

FALSE EVIDENCE APPEARING REAL

When you think something that is false is actually real—now *that's* crazy. It's basically the engine of the crazy train, and it's one of the Enemy's favorite strategies to get people stuck in fear. You see, one of the main reasons people become afraid in certain situations is that they see something, hear something, or experience something that serves as evidence that something is real, when it's not. The Enemy knows that once you believe something is real, it *is* real to you. But what's realer—the realest of all—is God and His Word. They bust the Enemy every time.

One of the best stories I know about this is one I wrote about in my book *Live Original.* I'll summarize it here to make the point that sometimes false evidence really does appear real, even to experts.

When we start thinking false evidence represents something real and we let that perceived reality cause fear to explode in our hearts and minds, we're headed in a dangerous direction.

Two-Mama noticed one day that I had a dark, round spot on one of my feet. After she asked me about it, I immediately became worried. A few days later, I asked a family friend who happened to be a doctor about it, and he suggested I get it checked out. I then showed it to another doctor friend of ours, who said it looked like something I had never heard of—a blue nevus, which is a kind of deep-skin mole—or perhaps some type of skin cancer, and that I should see a dermatologist. That *really* got my anxiety up!

The dermatologist said it definitely looked like a blue nevus and prepared to biopsy it to see if it was cancerous. At that point, I was almost paralyzed with fear. When the dermatologist began scraping the spot for the biopsy, it started fading and then it almost disappeared.

It was not a blue nevus. It was an ink spot from some dye

my friends and I had used for T-shirts. The dye was strong, so the spot hadn't come off even after days of soap and water.

I was terrified about that dark spot and what it could do to me. Three doctors looked at it, and it *appeared* to them to be a blue nevus. But it wasn't. The appearance was false. And that false appearance seemed real to the knowledgeable people around me. It was just enough to throw me into a major fear crisis. When the drama passed, I realized I never had anything to fear at all. Fear is like my blue-nevus-that-wasn't—false evidence appearing real. Big time. When we start thinking false evidence represents something real and we let that perceived reality cause fear to explode in our hearts and minds, we're headed in a dangerous direction.

WHEN THE EVIDENCE ISN'T FALSE

Before I go on, let me say that there is such a thing as a blue nevus. Most of the time it is not cancerous, but my dermatologist was wise to biopsy it anyway. Because of different things different people had said to me, and the fact that I let my thoughts run wild, I was so afraid I almost hyperventilated because of something that I should have been totally chill about. Had I known the truth, I could have stayed much calmer.

But what if it had been something bad? People are diagnosed with skin cancers all the time. People get terminally ill. People lose their jobs. Houses catch on fire. Teenagers become addicted to drugs. People we love pass away. All these things are real. They do happen, and the evidence supporting them is not false at all. It's real.

Gaining victory over fear does not mean that we can only be free from fear when something we think will be bad turns out to be okay, like my supposed blue nevus. It means we can stay brave, bold, confident, courageous, and strong in our faith in God whether a situation is a false alarm or the real thing. The Bible doesn't say, "Do not fear when something you thought would be scary isn't scary after all." It says, "Do not fear," period—and that even includes when you face real situations that truly can be frightening. That's when faith proves itself. That's when you get to show yourself and those around you how strong a person can be in Jesus and in the power of the Holy Spirit. As I've said before, to live fearless does not mean trying to find a way to make things not scary. It means looking the scary things in the eye and staring them down because God is in you and He is bigger than fear.

Check out this great quote from John Piper. It goes along perfectly with what I'm trying to say: "My feelings are not God. God is God. My feelings do not define truth.

God's word defines truth. My feelings are echoes and responses to what my mind perceives. And sometimes—many times—my feelings are out of sync with the truth."[1]

Gaining victory over fear means we can stay brave, bold, confident, courageous, and strong in our faith in God whether a situation is a false alarm or the real thing.

If you choose to accept the Enemy's lie and let him intimidate you with false evidence that appears real, or with something real that is genuinely frightening, you've bought yourself a ticket to the first stop on the crazy train.

WHAT IS THE CRAZY TRAIN AND WHERE IS IT GOING?

Before I define the crazy train, let me tell you how that image came about for me. One night my friend Brighton spent the night at my house. After we took off our makeup, we were sitting around talking and laughing, in our pajamas, just having fun like girls do. Before we knew it, we'd come up with a concept that describes the life cycle of fear. We weren't trying to do that. It just happened, and before long we realized we were on to something powerful—something that often has a major impact on people our age. We called it "the crazy train," and we posted about it on YouTube if you want to check it out.[2]

We started by asking the audience a series of questions we thought a lot of teenage girls could relate to, mostly about guys and boyfriend-girlfriend relationship stuff.

For example:

- Have you ever looked over your boyfriend's shoulder to see who he was texting?
- Have you ever seen a group text that you weren't part of and asked, *Why didn't they include me? Maybe they don't they like me anymore.*
- Have you ever looked at a group of people and seen them glance at you—and you immediately assumed they were talking about you?
- Have you ever called a friend five hundred million times because he or she didn't answer the first time? If you have ever *not* done that, you are amazing!
- Have you ever driven over to your boyfriend's

house at 8:00 in the morning because he didn't answer any of your calls or texts the night before?

Most of us have had some crazy thoughts and let our minds go some crazy places! (And done some crazy things too.) When Brighton and I were talking about these things (and yes, we had to admit at least one of us, probably both, had done all of them), we realized that what we were talking about could best be described as a crazy train.

The best way I can describe the crazy train is that it's a series of thoughts that takes you down a certain path in life. It's moving you in a specific direction—not necessarily a good one—and you just keep riding it. The way to stay on a crazy train is to keep thinking the way you're thinking, never entertaining the idea that you could take your life in a different direction if you'd simply change the way you think.

The best way I can describe the crazy train is that it's a series of thoughts that takes you down a certain path in life.

I heard Alex Seeley, pastor of the Belonging in Nashville, Tennessee, say something that explains this really well. She said that Satan is the Father of Lies, just like we read in John 8:44. When he lies to us, he often does it through our own thoughts. He'll plant a thought in our mind—something totally *not* true—and the next thing we know, we believe it! Alex said that the moment we come into agreement with that thought—that lie—is the moment we give the Enemy power in our lives. She's right! I've experienced that, but I never heard anyone articulate it so clearly until she did. That very first lie we believe, that moment we give power to the Enemy, is when we board the crazy train. When we believe the first lie, we make it easier for him to convince us of the second one, the third one, all the way to the end of the train.

FAIR WARNING

An old Japanese proverb says, "Fear is only as deep as the mind allows." That's true! The crazy train is made up of one wrong thought after another, one emotionally driven decision after another, one skewed perspective after another. When you're on it, people around you are saying, "Jump off! Jump off! Get yourself off that crazy train!" They can see that you're not thinking clearly, and they know you need to get off the train. But because you are so adamant that the direction your thoughts are taking you is the right one, you just stay on the train because you're thinking, *I can't jump off! I'm doing the right thing. Plus, jumping would be scary and it would hurt!*

The truth of the matter is, everything in your life would be so much better if you would just take the leap. Why? Because there's probably a big pile of emotional dynamite around the next bend in the tracks. The longer you stay on the train, the crazier things will get, and there's a good chance the whole situation will become really ugly before it's over.

While I was writing this book, I heard a pastor say something that fits perfectly in this chapter. He said that we all go through life doing what we think is best (sometimes that's how we end up on the crazy train). We're convinced that it's best, and we do not want anyone to talk us out of it. That's why when people tell us to get off the crazy train, we stick our fingers in our ears, look around randomly, and say, "I can't hear you."

The pastor went on to say that one reason we so often think we're right is that we can only see what we can see about our lives. We don't know what's coming around the next bend. God, however, sees the end from the beginning, and in His love, He guides us toward the end that He knows will be best for us, not the destination we think is right for us.

God can also see the big picture of our lives, while we are usually focused on smaller snapshots, like what's happening today, next week, next month, or next year. The pastor also noted that God often speaks to us with warnings. This could be an uneasy feeling on the inside, a thought that makes us want to change direction, or a person who says to us, "Get yourself off that crazy train!"

> When you find yourself on a crazy train, you don't see the whole picture of your life at any particular time.

The important point to remember when you find yourself on a crazy train is that you don't see the whole picture of your life at any particular time. Sometimes people who love you and care about you can see it more clearly than you do because they're not caught up in your swirling emotions. They're more objective. If they are urging you to get off the crazy train—or if what you're thinking about the direction in which you're headed does not align with God's Word—seriously consider heeding those warnings.

THE WORLD LOVES A CRAZY TRAIN

Crazy trains are a product of the world and of worldly thinking, not of God and godly thinking. The world loves a good crazy train and will do all it can to put you on one. By that I mean the world will say that stalking your boyfriend instead of building trust with him is okay. It will tell you that when your friends talk about you behind your back, ignore you, or leave you out of something, you deserve to be hurt—and not only that, you also have a right to seek revenge against them. The world will say that you should have a total freak-out when you see something frightening, hear bad news, or encounter a truly scary situation. It will tell you to take all your friends to dinner and buy their meals, plus appetizers and desserts if you are afraid they don't like you anymore (but that's not how you resolve relational issues; that's how you waste your money trying to buy friendship).

Thoughts and behaviors like these will only keep the crazy train going.

Did you notice that each situation I mentioned deals with relationships? That's because many of our problems in life, including our fears, are somehow rooted in relationships with others. The world can't teach us much about how to have godly relationships, so it's a good thing we have other options.

The best option I know of is the one Jesus talks about in Matthew 18, where He says, "If another believer sins against you, go privately and point out the offense. If the other person listens and confesses it, you have won that person back" (v. 15 NLT). If that doesn't work, He says to go to the person again, but this time, take one or two other people with you so they can hear what's being said (v. 16). If that isn't successful, then He says in in the next verse to get the church involved so the leaders there can help sort things out and bring reconciliation. After all these steps, if the person remains hard-hearted or stubborn, then He says it's okay to treat him or her "as a pagan or a corrupt tax collector" (v. 17). Hmm. In this passage, there's a *lot* of trying to work things out in an up-front way with people before treating them harshly.

One way to apply Matthew 18:15 in a practical way, for example, with a boyfriend you're afraid is being disloyal to you, would be to say something like, "Hey, I've just been wondering lately if you're texting other people or hanging out with other girls. Is that something I should be worried about?" and giving him a chance to tell you the truth about it. If you're right and he admits it, you can move on. If you're not, you'll know that you and he are fine, and you can resolve the situation.

The world can't teach us much about how to have godly relationships, so it's a good thing we have other options.

NOW THAT YOU UNDERSTAND THE CRAZY TRAIN

I could go on to say much more about the crazy train, but I hope showing the difference between the worldly way of doing things and Jesus' way was helpful to you. The world will always go one way, and Jesus will always have a better option.

Now let me bring us back to how the crazy train relates to fear. You've seen a train or a picture of a train before, so you know how trains work. The first part is the engine, then there are lots of different cars—perhaps passenger cars or cargo cars all hooked together—then a caboose. Without everything that follows the locomotive, there wouldn't be a train. It couldn't take people anywhere or transport goods from one place to another. It wouldn't really affect anybody. That's important, so stick with me.

When you have a fearful thought such as, *I'm afraid everyone's going to think I'm stupid because I failed chemistry,* that's fuel for the train. It's one fearful thought, and you get to choose whether or not cars (thoughts) can hook on to it. If you don't want to make a train, you think: *Okay, so I failed chemistry. It's a hard class. I'm not the first person who ever failed it, and I won't be the last. I'll have to retake it in summer school, but who knows, maybe*

I'll get to be good friends with someone else who failed it! It's not the end of the world.

If you do want to make a fear train, you start by adding this car: *What a disaster! I failed chemistry and everyone knows it. I'm so embarrassed that I have to go to summer school.* Then you hook on a thought like this: *I'm afraid I won't get into a good college. Both my parents are scientists, and I am scared they're going to punish me for not being good at chemistry. My sister made an A in it, and I'm scared she's going to make fun of me and call me an idiot.* Then you add something like this: *What if I fail another subject too? I mean, I never thought I'd fail chemistry, and look what happened! I'm afraid I'll never get out of high school! I'll never be able to do what I want to do in the future! My life is ruined!*

The world will always go one way, and Jesus will always have a better option.

By the time this person decides life has been ruined, the crazy train is moving full speed ahead, and they're well onboard. It ends in a meltdown, probably with tears, and the declaration that failing chemistry leads to no future whatsoever. The truth is, failing chemistry is not the best thing that can happen, but it's not the worst either. It's one class—and there's always summer school. The key to not letting one failing grade make you afraid that your life is over is to keep it in perspective and not add cars to the crazy train.

The same principle applies to any potentially frightening situation you could face. Whether it's your parents getting divorced, a grandparent who is sick, moving to a new city, a brother or sister who gets into major trouble—the scary scenarios are endless. You can start a crazy train with any of them. You can go all kinds of negative places with the scenarios you create in your mind. But please, *just don't.* Instead, remember that God is with you, that He has made you brave and strong, that people care about you, and that help is available.

Remember that God is with you, that He has made you brave and strong, that people care about you, and help is available.

HERE'S A QUESTION: Are you on a crazy train right now? Describe it.

HERE'S A CHALLENGE: I challenge you to jump off your crazy train. It'll take a lot of honesty and courage, but knowing what your train is and understanding that it isn't good for you will help you choose to get off.

HERE'S SOME ENCOURAGEMENT: Just jump. Whatever it takes for you to get off the crazy train, do it. I know it can be scary. I know it might hurt a little. But it'll be worth it, so go ahead and take the leap of faith.

HERE'S HOW YOU CAN PRAY: *Father, forgive me when my thoughts run wild, for I know that when You alone are my focal point, that's when I'll find peace. And please, give me the strength to jump off my crazy train!*

GET THE PEOPLE YOU CARE ABOUT OFF THEIR CRAZY TRAINS

Not only can you get off any crazy train you may be on right now, but you can also be the person who stands in the middle of the track and stops the crazy train for someone else. You can be the one yelling, "Jump off! Jump off! That train is crazy!"

It takes some maturity to help someone off the crazy train, especially when that person is controlled by fear. It's a lot easier to say to a friend who's afraid she's losing her friends, "Yeah, those girls probably were talking about you" than to say, "I don't know what they were talking about, but if it was about you, it had to be good!" It's easier to say to someone who is insecure about her boyfriend, "Yeah, I'll bet your boyfriend is cheating on you" than "He's never done anything to make you think you can't trust him. Give him the benefit of the doubt."

Instead of making a situation worse for someone, you can be the person who makes it better. When your friend starts moving down the crazy-train track, you can say, "Stop it right there! We don't know all the details or the context of what you saw, so let's not jump to conclusions." Or you can say, "I don't know how to solve this, but come on! We're getting off this train together because you don't need to be on it!"

When people around you are letting their feelings spin out of control and cause them to think, act, and speak in ways that aren't good for them, you can be the person who represents what is reasonable and what is true.

A good friend is one who stops a crazy train by saying something like, "Look, I understand exactly why you think this. I understand why you may be worried—because this is what you've seen or what you've heard. But

I'm going to tell you why you shouldn't get upset about it—because this is crazy and there's a better way to deal with it."

When people around you are letting their feelings spin out of control and cause them to think, act, and speak in ways that aren't good for them, you can be the person who represents what is reasonable and what is true. Be the one to say what God says while they are saying whatever their stirred-up feelings lead them to say. When they are overwhelmed with negative emotions such as fear, anxiety, anger, or hurt, overwhelm them with the Word of God. Remind them that God says they have a hope and a future (Jeremiah 29:11), that He loves them with an everlasting love that will never turn on them or fade away (Jeremiah 31:3), that He's always there when they call to Him (Psalm 55:16), and that He will never, ever, *ever* fail them or forsake them (Deuteronomy 31:6).

So-o-o . . .

* Fear starts in the mind and it generates emotions. One fearful thought will lead to another if you let it. The way to keep that from happening is to not allow yourself to camp out on fear in your mind.

- One of the Enemy's best tricks is to create fear by making false evidence appear real. No matter how things appear, God and His Word are what's true and real, and they will defeat the Enemy.
- One of the best things you can do for yourself is to get off the crazy train. One of the best things you can do for someone you love is to help them get off too.

Work the Word

The L*ORD* *is my rock, my fortress and my deliverer.*

2 Samuel 22:2

I know this verse is talking about the Lord as a rock, a fortress, and a deliverer, but when I read it I can't help thinking about dolphins and sharks. Let me explain.

I've heard a lot of stories about sharks trying to attack someone and dolphins swimming up to surround the potential victim, keeping that person safe and maybe even saving his or her life. It's like the dolphins form a fortress around the person, delivering them from injury or death.

My friend Laney is like that. I tell her all the time that she reminds me of a dolphin. When fear tries to attack someone, she has an amazing ability to surround that person with the truth of God's Word. She speaks the Word and the Word builds a fortress around the person—a fortress that fear can't get through. She's done that for me many times. She can sense when I feel nervous or anxious, or when a crazy train starts to form in my mind, and she'll say, "In the name of Jesus, you will *not* be afraid!" or something like, "Remember, Sadie, God has not given you a spirit of fear. He's given you power, love, and a sound mind" from 2 Timothy 1:7 NKJV.

As much as I value the fact that Laney does that for me, she's not always around when fear tries to sneak up on me. So I have to learn to fight fears with the Word at times on my own, without anyone's help. Let me encourage you to learn to do that too, speaking the Word to yourself and asking God to help it work on your mind and emotions.

You might also become the kind of friend to other people that Laney is to me. When you sense that they are feeling frightened or anxious, you can be the one to speak the Word and help them put it to work to push back the fear that threatens them.

5

Connect the Dots

Develop an attitude of gratitude, and give thanks for everything that happens to you, knowing that every step forward is a step toward achieving something bigger and better than your current situation.

Brian Tracy

I NEVER WAS VERY GOOD AT CONNECT-THE-DOT pictures, and I didn't enjoy doing them. I didn't have the patience for them, and I thought some of the dots were unnecessary. Give young Sadie a coloring book and a box of crayons any day, and definitely give me clothes so I can play dress up, but *please,* not a connect-the-dot drawing.

Now that I'm older, I still don't always like to connect the dots, but I have learned that doing it is not only important to living life well, it's necessary. If I want to be free, strong, and happy—living life with a sense of adventure and purpose—I can't draw my way around any of the dots life throws at me. I have to put my pencil firmly on the paper and drag it through them.

Though we can't see where life will take us, God can. And He knows every little dot we need to go through in order for the big picture to look like it's supposed to.

If you're wondering, *What on earth is she trying to say?* I can explain. Since I was, say, kindergarten age, I have not given one thought to connect-the-dot drawings. Zero. They were nowhere in my mind. But not long ago, it dawned on me that what God does in our lives is like those connect-the-dot pictures. He never shows us at the beginning of a journey what the end result will be. In fact, He doesn't even show us all the dots along the way. We often figure out what they are only when we find ourselves up against them. Wanting to know where we're ultimately going is human nature, but one beautiful thing about God is that He has a specific purpose for each of us, and He maps out our journeys so everything in our lives moves us closer to that purpose. But He doesn't give us a preview of the steps along the way.

Though we can't see where life will take us, He can. And He knows every little dot we need to go through in order for the big picture to look like it's supposed to. The dots are the places that challenge us and shape us. They're the things that will make us who we're meant to be and that give us the freedom and strength we need to live our very best lives. They have all kinds of names. There's the character-building dot, the grow-in-self-esteem dot, the realize-that-you're-unconditionally-loved dot, the learn-to-find-peace-in-life's-storms dot, the joy-is-everywhere-if-you-look-for-it dot, the make-Jesus-the-king-of-your-heart—no-*really* dot, and all kinds of others. The dot I went through before writing this book was the face-your-fears-and-find-your-freedom dot.

Chances are, you'll eventually realize that with God, there are no unnecessary dots.

Life's dots don't look like the polka dots on a Barbie doll dress, in perfectly coordinated colors and a pattern designed to catch the eye. Nope, they're much cruder than that. Some dots seem enormous and black, and you don't know if you'll ever find your way out of them. Some dots are smaller and easier to see your way through. As you get older, you'll look back on some of the dots as major crises in your life and on others as less dramatic learning experiences. And chances are, like me, you'll eventually realize that with God, there are no unnecessary dots.

HERE'S A QUESTION: What's your dot right now? What are you going through that feels hard or scary?

HERE'S A CHALLENGE: No matter how it feels, I challenge you to commit to going through the dot you're facing right now—all the way through it. Embrace it, deal with it, pray about it, and find Scriptures that will help you see it as God sees it and handle it in a godly way.

HERE'S SOME ENCOURAGEMENT: On the other side of your journey through your dot is something so amazing and so beautiful that it would break your heart to miss it. Working through your dot won't be easy, but God will help you and pour grace all over the process. And when you get that dot behind you, it will be awesome.

HERE'S HOW YOU CAN PRAY: *God, I want the big picture that You have in Your mind for my life to become a reality. Help me connect the dots and go through each one with the confidence that You are helping me, walking with me, fighting for me, healing me, and making me strong and free every step of the way.*

LOTS OF DOTS

When I was in school, I had to go through certain dots—such as learning how to be nice to people who were mean to me and having to study and do my homework when I wanted to be doing other things. Those are the fairly small dots in life, the ones most people have to deal with.

When *Duck Dynasty* came along, I faced other dots—ones I never imagined would touch my life. These included things such as losing a lot of my privacy, new levels of stress that came with having to balance activities I really enjoyed (like basketball and hanging out with friends) and what I needed to do (like go to school) with having to show up to film episodes. All that made my life and my schedule kind of crazy, but I learned to deal with it. I got through the dots.

When I appeared on *Dancing with the Stars,* I encountered yet another set of dots. For example, I forgot part of my dance one night. It was *terrible,* and I was convinced I had embarrassed myself in front of the whole world! I cried when it was over, and sometimes I cried just thinking about it.

Whenever I mentioned the mishap, people said, "Oh, I didn't even notice that!" or "Are you serious? You messed up? I couldn't tell!" Even my mom told me many times, "Sadie, no one saw it," and my mom always tells me the truth. But I knew what had happened and I thought surely everyone else was aware of it too. When people encouraged me to watch the episode so I could see for myself that it was hardly noticeable, I refused. *Why would I want to relive such a bad memory?* I thought. I chose instead to believe the lie that I made some kind of glaring mistake.

My friends and family tried to get me off that crazy train, but I was determined to stay on it. Eventually, I watched a video of the show—and the dance wasn't nearly as bad as I thought. My mom was right; people who didn't know how the steps were supposed to go had *no idea* I messed up. Once I saw the video, I felt much better about the whole situation. Getting through that dot took a while, but I'm glad I didn't stay stuck in feelings of guilt and shame.

When I was younger, the dots I went through affected what I was doing more than who I was. Naturally, from time to time, I went through periods of spiritual growth and the challenges that come with it. But the most stressful situations were what I would call *character building,* or lessons in learning to manage life. They didn't hit me at my core and tear me up inside the way another dot did. That dot was the hardest one *ever.* I'll tell you about it.

MY HARDEST DOT

It happened not long before I started writing this book. It was painful. But I want to share the story because I don't want the pain to be wasted. I want it to help other people, maybe even you.

I wrote about it in a blog titled "A Passionate Pursuit," which you can find it its entirety on liveoriginal.com. It's about a relationship that I thought was good but was actually quite stormy. Who the other person was and how long it lasted don't matter. What's important is what I learned during that time in my life and how God redeemed it. Here's how I described the situation and what God did for me in the midst of it.

I want to share the story because I don't want the pain to be wasted. I want it to help other people, maybe even you.

> We were so—"passionate"—and to me, it seemed like that could not possibly be a negative thing, because I heard the word *passion* at church all the time. The fact that I didn't fully understand the meaning of the word *passion* created so much confusion for me.

I thought our connection was so deep because we created this false love for ourselves that said it was okay to constantly fight like cats and dogs, scream hateful words, and cry until our eyes were swollen. All we'd have to do afterwards is share a kiss and make up. Then—boom!—our relationship would be stronger than ever. That was wonderful and all . . . until the next throw-down came, which was inevitably not too far around the corner.

We would go through this unhealthy pattern of "I hate you, I love you. I hate that I love you." The world makes that seem like such a normal, attractive cycle through its movies and music. But let me tell you, it definitely is not. We figured out the hard way that all it leaves you with is a lot of hurt, loneliness, and confusion.

You can go with the world's version of passion, which you'll see in the media, but I'm speaking from experience here when I say that even if it survives and the relationship lasts, you will be living for temporary moments of happiness and gratification instead of for true joy . . .

But things weren't always like that in the relationship. It wasn't always so volatile. At times, we knew how to have fun. We laughed uncontrollably, danced in public, and sang karaoke in the car. We ate ice cream and cooked pancakes before climbing on the rooftop to watch the stars say their final goodnight. We were free to be the best versions of ourselves around each other. And let me just say: I so adored him.

Over time, we welcomed sin into our relationship and allowed it to create a wedge between us and God. We unintentionally removed ourselves from the foundation of true love. God never moved or separated Himself from us; we simply tuned out truth and started walking down our own path. That is a dangerous, yet very common, thing to do.

Hindsight is 20/20, and when I look back, I know that God carried us both through everything. We were just too numb to feel His presence. I responded to the drama of our situation by burying myself in excuses and lies. Eventually I couldn't even remember the truth anymore.

One night after an intense fight that ended with the words, "I love you," something struck a chord in my heart. The word *love* awakened something in me. I had grown up in church. I knew that 1 Corinthians 13 talks about what love means. That day, the Holy Spirit led me to read that chapter again.

I clicked on a Bible app on my phone and began to read. That was when I decided to seek truth and invited God's words about love to tear down the wall of lies that had been building up for so long. I compared that interaction with the Word of God to a conversation I'd had with my boyfriend earlier that day. I realized my conversation with him was as far from "love" as anyone could possibly get.

I followed the voice of truth, realized that true passion isn't about drama (it's about intensity), and began a journey in pursuit of peace.

LACK OF PEACE = FAR FROM GOD

When I realized we had gotten to this point in our relationship, I knew I had to separate myself from it and get back to God—with my whole heart. It dawned on me: I had completely forgotten what peace felt like and that it was supposed to be part of my life. I had lived without it for so long—with unrest, discomfort, and a heavy, wrong-feeling heart on the inside—that I didn't even know I was missing it. I had gotten so far away from what the Bible said that I forgot to turn to it to look for the answers and direction I needed. Had I simply read a few key verses with an open heart to learn from them, I could have saved myself a lot of pain. I was settling for a life I thought I wanted, when God's Word said I could have something so much better. And the first part of "better" was to find peace.

One day, I got on my knees and prayed and read the Bible like I'd never read it before. God knew I was broken and sincere about returning to Him, and He activated His Word in my life that day in a way that has caused me to hunger for it, trust in it, and want to live by it in a way I never knew was possible. I asked Him to give me my peace back. He did, and He began to reveal His love to me in an incredibly powerful way. Once I connected the dots and realized that my lack of peace meant I was far from God, I repented, and He got busy redeeming the whole situation. Once I realized the problem and asked Him to get involved, He acted.

I could tell He did something in my heart, but I misinterpreted it. I thought that because I could feel a difference, I was finished with the situation. But there's more to the story. I'm going to stop it here for now, like television shows that say "To Be Continued" just when you *have* to know how things end. (I know, I'm dramatic sometimes.)

God's Word said I could have something so much better. And the first part of "better" was to find peace.

But until then, know that the day I decided I wanted my peace back was the day I ended the relationship that had been based on false passion. That put me on the journey with God that I'm on now, one that has had its ups and downs but keeps getting better and better.

I took a few detours in God's connect-the-dot picture, which messed up the drawing for a while. But once I turned my whole heart back to God, things began to change. Beauty returned.

I learned as I walked through my hardest dot that God is the One who lays out the dots of our lives. Our job isn't to figure out what the picture will ultimately look like; it's to walk where He leads. If you've ever done a real connect-the-dot picture, you know that sometimes you draw a line to the wrong dot, like I did. When you realize it, you erase it and make it right. But usually there's still a trace of the mark, and that helps you realize you didn't make the best decision. It's not that way with God. As my brother John Luke says, "God has a big eraser." And when God erases something, it's gone and the picture turns out perfectly.

I took a few detours in God's connect-the-dot picture, which messed up the drawing for a while. But once

I turned my whole heart back to God, things began to change. Beauty returned. The picture started looking better than ever.

It was like I was personally living the first verses of Psalm 30, where David says to God,

> You got me out of that mess. . . .
>   God, my God, I yelled for help
> and you put me together.
>   God, you pulled me out of the grave,
> gave me another chance at life
>   when I was down-and-out. (vv. 1–3 MSG)

Now, I feel like I'm living the last few verses of the psalm:

> I called out to you, God;
>   I laid my case before you . . . [saying,]
>   "So listen! and be kind! Help me out of this!"
> You did it: you changed wild lament
>   into whirling dance;
> You ripped off my black mourning band
>   and decked me with wildflowers.
> I'm about to burst with song. I can't keep quiet
>   about you.
>   God, my God, I can't thank you enough.
>   (vv. 8–12 MSG)

TAKE NOTE: No matter what you're going through or how you feel, there's probably something in the Psalms that describes it. David was a great warrior, king, and leader, but he went through a *lot*! Everything about his life was not easy, and he made some big mistakes. He wasn't always faithful to God, but the psalms he wrote show us that he realized God was faithful to him. Here are some psalms that might be appropriate for whatever you're going through right now. Which one suits you best?

- Psalm 32
- Psalm 40
- Psalm 46
- Psalm 51
- Psalm 130

WHEN YOUR FEAR BECOMES YOUR FAVORITE

While I was writing this book, I heard something intriguing. I spoke at an event with several world-class gymnasts. We're talking about names you would know, people you've seen on Olympic podiums with medals around their necks.

At this event, the audience had a chance to ask the gymnasts questions. A little girl asked this: “What’s the scariest thing you’ve ever done in gymnastics?” (I was sitting there thinking, *Great question. I can’t wait to hear the answers.*) The girl was basically asking them to talk about their hardest dot, as I’d put it.

I was fascinated by the gymnasts’ responses. Each one had a story to tell about a scary move, and several of them said they were so frightened of those particular moves because they had been hurt doing them before. So of course they were scared! They didn’t want to sprain another ankle, do another face-plant, fall off a balance beam, or miss the high bar and end up in a pile underneath it. Since they had been injured before, the one thing they wanted to avoid was getting hurt again.

I understood all of that, but it’s not what really caught my attention. At the end of their comments, they *all* made essentially the statement: the element they were most afraid of eventually became their favorite one to do. Why? Because they chose to go through those most frightening and most difficult dots; they kept trying and kept practicing until they were no longer afraid and they mastered them. Once they mastered them, they loved doing what they once hated. All because they faced their dots head-on, chose not to be afraid of them anymore, and conquered them.

The Enemy is afraid of your becoming everything God wants you to be.

A philosopher named Eric Hoffer called himself an atheist, but he wrote something that I think reveals an important truth about the Christian life: "You can discover what your enemy fears most by observing the means he uses to frighten you."[1] To put this thought in a Christian context, the Enemy is afraid of your becoming everything God wants you to be. Because he's afraid of that, he tries to make you afraid of it too. If you can identify what the Enemy wants you to fear, that's the very thing you need to go after with faith.

Going back to the story from my blog, near the end of it, I wrote a prayer for my future husband. The Enemy had tried to discourage me in all kinds of ways by using that tumultuous relationship against me. I take full responsibility for the bad choices I made, but in the end, like all of us, I also have to make the choice to believe that what I long for can come true.

I've decided to take the risk and not be afraid of another relationship. I believe God will use the lessons I learned from that painful relationship in a redemptive way in the future. I am no longer afraid. God gave me the strength to walk through that dot, and the fact that I am open to another relationship in His perfect timing with the right person proves that dot is now behind me. When we deal in a healthy way with what once caused fear, pain, shame, disappointment, anger, or other negative emotions, it becomes a place of strength and happiness, a beautiful picture with all the dots connected.

HERE'S A QUESTION: What causes you more fear than anything else?

HERE'S A CHALLENGE: You know what this challenge is going to be. You know that thing I just asked you about, the one that causes you more fear than anything else? I challenge you to face it.

HERE'S SOME ENCOURAGEMENT: I'm pretty sure the Olympic gymnasts would join me in encouraging you to take a deep breath and jump into the very thing you fear most. They've done it. I've done it, and I know you can too! Trust them and trust me: once you finally do, it will be so great that you'll wonder why you waited so long.

HERE'S HOW YOU CAN PRAY: *Lord Jesus, I pray that I would see evidence of Your love in the midst of my biggest fears and that You would give me the courage to risk doing what I am afraid of.*

So-o-o . . .

* The most important point in this chapter is that everything in life doesn't feel great all the time. Those are the dots you'll need to go through as God draws the amazing masterpiece He wants to create in your life.
* You always have the option to avoid the dots, but it's not a good idea. The thing to do is take a deep breath and face them head-on. Wrap yourself in courage and faith, like you would slip on a jacket before you step out into a big storm. Then take the first step to deal with your dot, then another, then another.
* At just the right moment, you'll realize that dot is now behind you. And you've stepped into something amazing. What you once feared may become your very favorite thing.

Work the Word

Was not even Rahab the prostitute considered righteous for what she did when she gave lodging to the spies and sent them off in a different direction?

James 2:25

You know what the Enemy does sometimes? He puts fear in you—fear that you aren't good enough, that maybe God doesn't really love you, that even though His Word works for everyone around you, it won't work for you. He'll even ask you the question "Who are *you* to try to speak the Word and apply it to your life?" That's why I love James 2:25: this verse blows the Enemy's lies to pieces.

Rahab, as the verse says, was a prostitute. In most people's opinion, especially during the time she lived, prostitution was not an honorable or righteous profession. But James doesn't say anything about that. He says that she was "considered righteous" because she helped God's people back when they were trying to enter the promised land.

God saw what was good about Rahab, not what was bad about her. He looked for a reason to consider her righteous, not to label her a sinner. He's the same today. You and I have done things we may be ashamed of, things not viewed as righteous, but when we are in Christ, they are covered by His blood and washed away. When God sees us as His children, He sees through the eyes of perfect, unconditional love everything good about us.

I want to encourage you to always remember this verse. When you feel like you aren't good enough or worthy enough, defeat that lie by saying, "I know James 2:25, and if Rahab was good enough, so am I!"

6

Exhale Your Ugly

In the process of telling the truth about what you feel or what you see, each of us has to get in touch with himself or herself in a really deep, serious way.

June Jordan

HAVE YOU EVER HAD A TIME IN YOUR LIFE when you just felt ugly? Maybe it was because you had a breakout, or you got a bad haircut, or that outfit you thought would look so good on you doesn't really look good on you at all.

We all know the kinds of ugly I'm talking about. Once, when I was in high school, I got the worst haircut ever. I didn't like the way my hair fell in my eyes as I ran up and down the basketball court, so I called my hairdresser to ask for a quick trim. She couldn't do it, and neither could anyone else I knew. Our team was scheduled to start a tournament the next day, and I thought I *had* to have a trim. So I went to the hair salon in a big discount store thinking, *How bad could it be? It's just a little trim to get my hair out of my eyes.*

In this chapter, I'm talking about a different kind of ugly—the kind you feel when it's happening on the *inside*. I'm talking about fear, anger, resentment, and jealousy.

Let me tell you, it was *bad.* On one side of my head, the girl took off one inch of my hair. On the other side, she cut four inches! It looked horrible, and I cried the entire rest of the day. You know that old saying, "You get what you pay for"? Well, the total price of the haircut was five dollars. I learned the hard way what five dollars will get you in a hair salon—and it's not pretty!

I've had plenty of other experiences that made me feel ugly on the outside, and perhaps you have too. But in this chapter, I'm talking about a different kind of ugly—the kind you feel when it's happening on the *inside.* I'm talking about fear, anger, resentment, jealousy—all those negative emotions that cause you to think you're weak, unimportant—and yes, ugly—and that you have no future.

The thing about all of this is that when something is ugly on the outside, people can see it and we're embarrassed about it. But when the ugly is on the inside, no one can see it and we're alone with it. We are more likely to deal with ugly on the outside because we want others to stop looking at it. The embarrassment we feel motivates us to fix the problem. But when we think we are the only ones who can see the ugly on the inside, we're easily tempted to let it sit in the dark places inside of us, where it grows and gets worse. It's a lot better to be embarrassed about ugly on the outside than it is to be alone wrestling with something ugly on the inside.

When you feel ugly on the outside, you can clear up the breakout, let your hair grow, or exchange an outfit that doesn't look good for one that does. When you feel ugly on the inside, none of those strategies will work. When the problem is on the inside, the solution has to start on the inside too. You have to do what I call "exhale your ugly."

I've had a lot of practice exhaling my ugly. Not long before I started writing this book, I went through about a two-year season of ugly. And I can assure you, it took a lot of exhaling to get all that ugly out!

Before we go any further, let me explain what I mean by "exhaling your ugly." Think about the way you breathe. You take air into your body when you inhale, and when you exhale, you let it out. You release the air you've been holding inside. So when I say, "Exhale your ugly," I'm talking about letting go of negative emotions like fear, disappointment, and all the things that make you feel ugly and unworthy. You just release all of that pain and roll it over to God. It's just like 1 Peter 5:7 says, "Give all your worries and cares to God, for he cares about you" (NLT).

I've had a lot of practice exhaling my ugly.

EXHALING MY PERSONAL UGLY

Exhaling my ugly started on January 16, 2017—the beginning of the forty-six-city Winter Jam tour. I sat in a hotel room at a beautiful beach resort, and I wept. Now, if you have ever been to a perfect beach, you know that it's not a place where you want to sit in your hotel room crying!

But no matter how much the sand and waves called to me, I stayed right there on my bed, crying. The tears were welcome because for nearly a year prior to that day—since the breakup—I had not been able to cry. I had held a lot of pain and regret in my heart and hidden it from everyone around me. I even tried to hide it from God because, even though I had learned years ago in Sunday school that God sees and knows everything, I didn't want Him to see the hurt swirling in my heart. I was running from Him as hard as I could, trying to hide my ugly so He wouldn't see it. I shut down my feelings where He was concerned, sucked everything up, and put on my game face, which did not allow for tears. Like the children playing on the beach outside my window, burying their toys in the sand and then using their little shovels to unearth them, I had buried many hurtful things deep in the sand of my heart, hoping to keep them out of sight and out of mind. I was so ashamed that I never told *anyone* about those hurtful things. I thought that if I buried them so deeply that I couldn't see them, they wouldn't hurt me anymore, right? No! I found out that day that ignoring the pain we bury is completely wrong. The hurts we try to cover up in our hearts get infected and inflamed, and they affect us in negative ways, even when we do not realize it.

I wept that day because I finally figured out something really important. Actually, *I* didn't figure it out; the Holy Spirit revealed to me. I realized that during my time of trying to hide from God, I never stopped praying. I still believed in Him and still knew I needed Him; I just didn't want to get Him involved in certain areas of my

I was running from God as hard as I could, trying to hide my ugly so He wouldn't see it.

life at that time. So I prayed prayers like this: "God, when I go out to speak tonight, give me wisdom to know what to say. Help me do a good job encouraging the audience in their faith . . ." I knew I was spending time in prayer (that's good, right?), but I had no idea I was completely ignoring the pain in my heart. I wanted God to help me function well on the outside, but I wasn't inviting Him into my inside.

When the dam holding back my ugly emotions finally burst that January day, I bawled. I wept because I realized I had been praying about my present without having dealt with my past—the mistakes, the pain, and the words running around in my brain—negative words and lies I had spoken to myself, and others had spoken to me. Without realizing it, I had started to believe those words, and I had come into agreement with the Father of Lies. A lot of us do that every day. We agree with the lie that tells us we aren't good enough. We believe the lie of shame, the lie of guilt, the lie of resentment, the lie of rejection. The list goes on.

Proverbs 18:21 says, "The tongue has the power of life and death, and those who love it will eat its fruit." This

We agree with the lie that tells us we aren't good enough. We believe the lie of shame, the lie of guilt, the lie of resentment, the lie of rejection.

means that words can cause things to come alive in us or cause things to die in us. Some of the words that had been spoken to me were causing parts of my heart to get ugly and die. Part of breaking free from the pain of my past meant dealing with those words and their impact. Before the end of this chapter, I'll write about how I did it so that if you have also believed lies and they have brought pain and ugliness into your heart, you can find freedom too.

When I realized I had been praying for my present without asking God to heal the pain of my past, that's when things began to change. The Holy Spirit showed me that unless I dealt with the hurts I still carried from the past, I would not be able to totally enter into and enjoy the future He has for me. This meant that I needed to admit my hurts honestly to Him, hold nothing back, and allow myself to feel the pain they caused; then I needed to release it all to Him, ask Him to heal it, and receive His healing work. That's what it took to exhale my ugly.

I've learned since that time that holding on to ugly on the inside blinds us to the beauty that's around us. It's not that beauty isn't there; it's that we can't see it. The whole time I was praying, God was there for me. I know He was listening to my prayers. I could have tapped into the beauty that was waiting for me in Him, but I didn't—yet.

That January day in the hotel room, I got out a notebook and started writing down everything that was hurting me beneath the surface of my life, all those things I had buried in the sand. At that point, I didn't know what would happen. I knew I needed to get them out of the pit of my soul, but as I looked at my list I had to ask myself, "Will these things always have a hold on me?"

I hoped not, so I kept writing, praying with each word to find freedom somehow. When I finished, there was no bolt of lightning from heaven, no voice of God from the clouds pronouncing my release from the pain, no visit from an angel who bandaged the wounds of my heart and told me everything would be okay. Hate to break it to you, but nothing happened—but I did confess my pain in writing. I got it out of me, but I wasn't sure where it went. I felt a little better, but not all the way better until later.

BREAKTHROUGH!

Three months went by, and I continued to pray about my past because I understood that the only thing holding me back from my future was the fact that I was holding on to my past. On April 30, I went to visit my mentor.

Before I write about what happened during my time with her, let me say that I could have talked to any number of friends about this situation, and I knew that friends would listen and maybe validate my feelings or tell me what I wanted to hear. That's what friends often do, but it wasn't what I needed at that time. A godly mentor will provide three things friends don't always offer: (1) A godly mentor will not judge. (2) That person will not validate feelings that don't align with God's Word. (3) He or she will cover the lies you've believed with God's truth.

Once I sat down face-to-face with my mentor, I suddenly felt an overwhelming conviction to share with her the pain that had hurt me and had been hiding inside of me, holding my heart captive.

As I talked to her and began to tell her how I felt about things deep in my soul, how I'd tried to run and hide from God, how ashamed I was, and what kinds of lies people had spoken about me, she listened. And then she did the most amazing thing: she simply began to speak

A godly mentor will provide three things friends don't always offer:

1. A godly mentor will not judge.
2. That person will not validate feelings that don't align with God's Word.
3. He or she will cover the lies you've believed with God's truth.

truth from the Word of God. Her knowledge of the Word is incredible, and every verse or biblical principle she shared with me brought light into my heart where darkness had lived for a long time. As she shared the Word and prayed for me and with me, I began to find freedom. I could see the lies for what they were—complete untruth.

As the Word of God brought light to my mind, those lies began to unravel and no longer held me captive. I realized that the exercise of writing down my pain on paper was important, but it was only the first step. I was trying to find freedom in words that I had written, but freedom is only found in the words *God* has written. It was not until I spoke those words, took their authority in

Jesus' name, and began to speak what God has said, that healing began to come. On paper, those words and feelings were still in hiding, but when they came out of my mouth, all that ugly finally got exposed.

Eventually all the pain my mentor helped me release became a passion for me. Part of that passion is to use the pain I experienced and the freedom I found to help you release your pain and be set free.

In the weeks and months following that, I started to feel like plankton. With the Holy Spirit's grace and with my mentor's help, I began to see a new side of God and to develop a deeper relationship with Him. I drifted back to the light, so to speak. And after all that pressure, I began to glow. Psalm 34:5 describes perfectly what happened: "Those who look to him are radiant; their faces are never covered with shame." The key to breakthrough, though, is looking to Him. That's where healing is.

My journey from finally breaking down in tears of desperation in a hotel room to an amazing experience of healing and freedom didn't just happen. In order for change to come *to* my life, I had to change some things *about* my life. If you are wondering if you can ever find freedom from your pain, I encourage you to start by looking to God and to God alone. I don't know what your journey will be, but I believe with all my heart that God has freedom for you and that you will find it.

HERE'S A QUESTION: Do you have some personal ugly that needs to be exhaled? Today can be the day you finally let it go. Will you do it?

HERE'S A CHALLENGE: Believe me, I know that exhaling your ugly can be really hard and sometimes even scary, but I also know it's worth it. I challenge you to go ahead and do it. Let go of all that pain and fear.

HERE'S SOME ENCOURAGEMENT: The feeling of cleanness and beauty you will have after you do it is even better than you can imagine. Once you've exhaled your ugly, you'll be in a whole new place with God. You'll feel tons better about yourself and about your future. Just think about what it would be like to live without all that heaviness on the inside. A whole new level of freedom is within your reach!

HERE'S HOW YOU CAN PRAY: *God, break my heart for what breaks Yours—and when I try to hide from You the things that are hurting me, I believe that breaks Your heart. I pray that You would show up in power in my life, right where I need You most. I pray that wherever I go, I will sense Your presence. Keep my focus on You and You alone. Help me understand deep in my heart that I am loved, beautiful, and more valuable than I can imagine—no matter what I have been through in the past. I pray for freedom from my pain. Help me to exhale my ugly. I want to experience the beauty I know is in Your presence.*

TAKE NOTE: I wrote in this chapter about 1 Peter 5:7: "Give all your worries and cares to God, for he cares about you" (NLT). Why don't you take a few minutes now and write down all your worries and cares? When you finish, pray over each one and release it to God—a big emotional exhale.

SEVEN STEPS TO EXHALE YOUR UGLY

Exhaling my ugly was such a turning point in my life that I really want to make sure you know specifically what to do if you want to do the same.

The old saying "Time heals all wounds" is not true. Time does not heal. Jesus heals, and He heals in the ways and according to the timing that is right for each person.

Here are seven steps I took to deal with my ugly; I think they will help you deal with yours. Before I share them,

I also want to say that this is not some kind of formula that automatically works, and it's not on a schedule. In many ways, I'm still on my journey of healing, but a lot of my healing was concentrated in that three-month period between mid-January and the end of April. It doesn't work that way for everyone. The important thing is for you to find the timing God has for *your* healing and go along with that. The old saying, "Time heals all wounds" is not true. Time does not heal. Jesus heals, and He heals in the ways and according to the timing that is right for each person.

I can't promise that if you take these seven steps you will immediately get the breakthrough you long for. But I can promise that if you use them as a general guide and follow the Holy Spirit as He guides you, He will ultimately lead you to the breakthrough that will change your life.

1. PRAY LIKE CRAZY. As I mentioned earlier in this chapter, even during the most miserable, most painful time of my life, I prayed. I wasn't praying as I should have been, but I was praying all I knew to pray. I believe God knew I was crying out to Him, even though He would soon lead me to pray differently. Romans 8:26–27 says,

> The Holy Spirit helps us in our weakness. For example, we don't know what God wants us to pray for. But the Holy Spirit prays for us with groanings that cannot be expressed in words.

> And the Father who knows all hearts knows what the Spirit is saying, for the Spirit pleads for us believers in harmony with God's own will. (NLT)

These verses give me incredible comfort, and I hope they also encourage you. God knows your heart. When He sees that you want His help to exhale your ugly, He'll give you all the help you need. Don't worry about getting the words exactly right when you pray; the Holy Spirit will take care of that. Just be sure you are praying and sharing your heart with God.

As you go through the following steps to exhale your ugly, it's important that before, during, and after each one, you pray like crazy. Cover each of these steps in prayer, asking God to help you along the way. When God helps you with every step, you're guaranteed to end up in the right place at the end of your journey. And that's a new level of beauty, confidence, freedom, wholeness, and love.

2. TELL YOURSELF THE TRUTH. I found this quote from an unknown author, and I think it's amazing: "In a time of universal deceit, telling the truth is a revolutionary act." Part of exhaling your ugly is finally telling yourself, God, and other trustworthy people the truth about the ugliness in your heart, your mind, and your life. I've got firsthand experience with that. One lesson I've learned is that you can't tell the truth to God or to others until you

first tell it to yourself. You have to admit to yourself that you are scared of something (or even totally consumed by fear), hurt by something someone said or did to you, disappointed, angry—or whatever you feel.

Christians get with God and let Him lead them as they deal with negative, destructive emotions—including fear. Then they receive His healing and move forward.

If you were raised to believe that "real Christians" don't have bad feelings, let me drop a truth bomb on you: that is simply not right. "Real Christians" do have bad feelings sometimes because they are part of being human. Christians just get with God and let Him lead them as they deal with those negative, destructive emotions—including fear. Then they receive His healing and move forward.

Nothing's going to happen on the healing journey unless you first tell "the truth, the whole truth, and nothing but the truth" to yourself. You have to know and own where you are in your life if you ever want to move beyond it.

3. GET YOUR PAIN OUT. Once you've been brutally honest with yourself, find a way to get the pain out of your

heart. For me, that meant writing down everything that had hurt me, disappointed me, made me afraid, or made me angry—plus everything that I was embarrassed to admit. I held nothing back. That same exercise of writing things down might work for you too. It's also okay if you express yourself in some other way—like with a drawing or a painting, a dance, a song or poem, kickboxing, or some other way of releasing what's bottled up inside of you. The important thing is to stop trying to hide your hurts. It's time to bring them into the light. Remember, just letting your pain out doesn't bring freedom. That's why the next step matters so much.

4. ASK GOD TO HEAL YOU. Telling God about your pain is just the beginning. Asking God to heal you is what moves you forward. I've already encouraged you to cover the whole process of exhaling your ugly with prayer. In this step, I'm talking about just letting it all out and then saying something like, *So God, I'm just asking You to heal me.* If you wrote down the things that trouble you, like I did, you could get that list and say something like, *Okay, God, these are my problems. I know You already know more about them than I do, but it's important to me to share them with You and invite You to get involved in my life and set me free from them.* Or *God, this pain is so deep, it's hard for me to believe it will ever heal, but I know that You are the Healer. So I'm going to let You have it, and I'm*

asking You to do what You need to do. Once you sincerely surrender your situation to Him and ask Him to help you, you'll begin to see Him working in new ways in your life.

5. SHARE YOUR HEART WITH SOMEONE YOU TRUST. I mentioned earlier that even when I wrote down all the things I was struggling with, I didn't feel like anything really changed until I shared with my friend what I was going through. James 5:16 talks about this: "Confess your sins to each other and pray for each other so that you may be healed. The earnest prayer of a righteous person has great power and produces wonderful results" (NLT). I don't know how to make this point any better than James did. I just know from experience that the game-changer for me as I exhaled my ugly was to talk it over with someone I trusted and to have that friend pray with me and for me. That's when the "wonderful results" started happening!

6. OPEN YOUR HEART TO HEALING. Just as a good parent would never leave a child lying on the ground bleeding after falling off a bicycle or standing there crying after slamming a finger in a car door, God doesn't want to leave you alone in your pain. But sometimes, especially when shame has gone deep, we want to hide from God. We might finally get our pain out, and then go into hiding again for a while.

Embrace the healing God wants to bring.

Embracing the healing God wants to bring us is not always easy. So how to do we do it? We simply make a choice and say something like this to God (and mean it): *God, I don't know what Your healing will look like in my life, but I choose to open my heart to whatever You need to do to make me whole and strong.*

7. BELIEVE GOD'S WORD. Nothing will change your life like God's Word. It has the power to make you feel beautiful where you once felt ugly, to replace feelings of worthlessness with confidence of your value to God, and to strengthen you where you once felt weak. It's the most effective weapon on earth to defeat the lies the world tries to get you to believe. I've listed on the next pages a few of my favorite powerful pieces of God's Word.

Let me warn you: these words can't do much for you if all you do is scan them quickly and then check your social media. But if you will read them slowly, with your heart and mind open, as though they are written especially for you, like they are truth (because they are), and like they really mean what they say for you personally (because

If you *really* think about God's Word and apply it to your circumstances, it will change your life.

they do)—if you really think about them and apply them to your circumstances—then they will change your life. If you will ask the Holy Spirit to enlighten your spiritual eyes and help you understand what God's words mean to you personally, and then ask yourself, "If I really believed these words, how different would my life be?" I think you may be shocked (in a good way!).

Now to the words themselves. Before each verse, I'll summarize the lies the world wants you to believe, and then I'll immediately share a truth from the Word that will knock the breath out of that lie.

> *The world says:* "You're not valuable. Nobody really cares about you, and no one ever will."
>
> *But God's Word says:* "Look at the birds of the air; they do not sow or reap or store away in barns, and yet your heavenly Father feeds them. Are you not much more valuable than they?" (Matthew 6:26).

> *The world says:* "No one will ever love you or respect you. You don't matter to anyone."
>
> *But God's Word says:* "Since you are precious and honored in my sight, and because I love you, I will give people in exchange for you, nations in exchange for your life" (Isaiah 43:4).

The world says: "You'll never amount to anything. There's just too much wrong with you!"

But God's Word says: "Even before he made the world, God loved us and chose us in Christ to be holy and without fault in his eyes" (Ephesians 1:4 NLT).

The world says: "You never do anything right!"

But God's Word says: "I can do all this through him who gives me strength" (Philippians 4:13).

The world says: "You will never overcome your weaknesses. You're stuck with them, and you can't get away from them."

But God's Word says: "[God] said to me, 'My grace is sufficient for you, for my power is made perfect in weakness.' Therefore I will boast all the more gladly about my weaknesses, so that Christ's power may rest on me" (2 Corinthians 12:9).

These aren't verses to simply read and pray over today while you're reading this book. Instead, while you're sitting in your room (or wherever) right now, speak the words of the verses above. *Say what God says.* I mean it. These words of life will keep you grounded in how God views you and thinks about you for the rest of your life. If you want to embrace the beauty He sees in you, keep them on your mind and in your heart as often as possible, return to them often, memorize them, think about them, and let them become the foundation of your self-image. When that happens, you won't have any more room for ugly.

So-o-o . . .

* Everybody has some ugly. It may be hurt feelings, disappointment, negative words you've spoken to yourself or others have spoken about you, or crippling fear that's keeping you from moving forward in your life. Whatever your ugly is, it's time for a big exhale.
* Exhaling your ugly isn't comfortable, pleasant, or easy. But it's worth it because whole new levels of freedom, faith, confidence, and beauty are waiting for you on the other side.
* Here are seven steps to exhale your ugly: pray like crazy, tell yourself the truth, get your pain out, ask God to heal you, share your heart with someone you trust, open your heart to healing, and believe God's Word.

Work the Word

I have hidden your word in my heart
that I might not sin against you.
Psalm 119:11

I heard a story about God speaking to a missionary, telling him to learn His Word well because there would come a day when he would not be able to have his Bible anymore. The man took seriously that message and began studying and memorizing Scripture as hard as he could.

Years passed and the man was captured during a time of war. Just as God had told him, he found himself without access to a Bible. But because he had learned and studied so many verses and passages of Scripture, he could remind himself of them.

While he was in prison, someone was able to get one page of a Bible, and the prisoners passed it around to each other. I can only imagine how valuable it was to them!

I don't think anyone could ever understand how truly important the Word is until they need and don't have it. When we need to work the Word and we don't have it hidden in our hearts so we can quickly call it to mind, that's a very unfortunate situation. I really want to encourage you not only to read the Scriptures from your Bible or on your phone or tablet but also to memorize them.

Having the Word in our hearts and minds not only keeps us from sinning against God, as Psalm 119:11 says, it also strengthens us when we feel weak, gives us courage when we are afraid, and gives us peace when everything around us seems out of control. Hide the words of Scripture in your heart, so you'll always have them with you and the Word can work on you at any time, in any place.

7

A Champion or a Legend?

You don't have to look like a champion to be a legend.

Me (Sadie)

I WAS ONCE VISITING A LARGE, PRESTIGIOUS Christian university and a good friend of mine said, "Sadie, I've got a friend I really need you to talk to. His name is Taylor." Taylor said he had been a Christian earlier in his life, but he had become an atheist. In reality, I'm not sure that's totally accurate because he did believe that God exists. He was just running from God, from church, and from his Christian friends. Big-time.

When I met Taylor, I thought, *All right, no pressure. God will help me with this.*

We started talking, and I quickly began to notice something. He was choosing the short straw in every area of his life. What I mean by "the short straw" is that he continually chose to look at what was negative about his life, not what was positive. He had locked his focus onto his problems instead of his potential.

You see, Taylor was deaf when he was younger, but when I met him he could hear because of an implant. Still, he was angry with God for "doing that to me," he said. He also told me that he struggled with not being able to see God (as in, God is invisible), so he said, "How could I possibly believe in Him?"

I responded, "So are you saying you're upset with God because of the deafness, and yet you don't believe in God because you cannot see Him?"

"Yes," he answered.

All I could think of to say was, "Okay. So do you believe in fear?"

Again, he answered, "Yes."

Obviously, he did believe in things he could not see. He trusted that fear exists, even though he couldn't see it. But he did not trust that God exists when he couldn't see Him.

> I told him, "God is just as real as the fear is."

When I pointed out to Taylor that he *did* believe in something he could not see, he had to agree. We kept talking and realized he believed completely in his fear of other people—and he let that fear control him. I understood that the fear was real, so I told him, "God is just as real as the fear is."

He didn't stop there, though. He went on to say more about being afraid of other people. As it turned out, that fear was based in what he perceived to be his greatest weakness, his struggle to speak properly. Because he felt his speech was not quite normal, he did not want to talk to other people.

There was the rub. A lot of his problem was rooted in the way he felt about how he spoke. You see, when he had surgery to place the implant in his ear, it did give him the ability to hear, but when he woke up from the operation and began talking, his speech sounded unusual, and he suddenly found speaking difficult. I guess he felt like he traded one physical challenge for another, and he was bitter about it.

I shared with him, "Taylor, the Enemy is the one who has defined your speech as your weakness. That belief is not from God. I truly believe God has always intended for your words to be your strength. And that's what He still intends for you now. I think you need to flip your script because you have just as much power to believe the Enemy as you have to believe God. You can believe either one, and you have repeatedly believed the wrong one. You keep choosing the opposite of what God wants you to believe. You can see the cross of Christ as a place of death or as a point of victory." Once he realized that he was strong in his own way and not weak, as other people thought, he came back to the Lord.

Taylor is now on solid spiritual ground and continually growing as a Christian. He is president of his fraternity, and he gives speeches in front of the whole school! God really did want to take what Taylor saw as weakness and turn it into strength.

Aren't we all a bit like that in certain ways? We may not have turned our backs on God or embraced atheism, but most of us have allowed the Enemy to convince us to believe certain negative things about ourselves. Those beliefs have caused us to struggle, sometimes terribly or for quite a long time. All along, if we would simply listen to God and align our thoughts with His thoughts, we would see that those areas represent our greatest strengths, our highest potential, and our divine destiny.

FIFTH-GRADE GYM CLASS

Don't forget about Taylor, but for a moment, let's set up a situation to which we can all relate. You're back in fifth grade gym class and the PE teacher says it's time to pick teams for dodgeball. Did the very thought of that scenario cause anxiety for you? It does for some people!

Let's say you do a lot of things well. You're smart. You make good grades. You can play the guitar like nobody's business, and you have a great personality. But you are *not* an athlete. You feel you have no sports ability whatsoever. Your heart sinks because you know you will be the last person chosen for a team, and you just pray you get on the right team. You know what I mean. You want to be on the team with the most athletic guy in your class, the one who always leads everyone else to victory. He's the guy who has worn athletic gear to school since prekindergarten, the first one to make a three-pointer, and the one who always beat everyone else in the hundred-yard dash. In a word, he was the stud. Naturally, you want to be on his team because, no doubt, his team will win.

But you don't get picked for his team. (Hey, he knows athleticism when he sees it—and when he looks at you, he doesn't see it). Instead, you get picked for the worst team in the history of the world. The one with a full roster of athletes like, well, you.

Goliath is the champion and David becomes the legend.

Now that you have that situation in your mind and you're

remembering the feelings that go with it, let me say that it reminds me of a modern-day twist on a story you may have heard before. The story of my friend Taylor reminds me of it too. I'm talking about the dramatic tale of David and Goliath—a battle between Goliath, a Philistine hero with a very sharp sword and body-builder muscles to swing it, and a pipsqueak of a boy named David, with a nothing but a slingshot. I'm going to spend most of the rest of this chapter writing about David and Goliath in detail—and if you want to read even more about it, I highly recommend Louie Giglio's book *Goliath Must Fall*—but for now let me just say that the fight between the two of them became the story of a champion versus a legend. It probably goes without saying, but Goliath is the champion and David becomes the legend.

You may think a champion and a legend would be fairly similar. Often, in conversation, we say things like, "Did you see that touchdown he scored when he won the game for us? It was awesome! He's a legend!" Or "Seriously, you made a hundred on that algebra test? It was *so* hard! You're brilliant! You're a legend!" In circumstances like these, we use the word *legend,* but what we really mean is *champion.*

The words do have some similarities. Otherwise, we wouldn't confuse them so often. But one carries much more weight than the other. With one, you win a trophy.

With the other, you win a legacy. With one, when the spotlight fades from you, you drop the microphone and move on. With the other, you pass the mic from generation to generation. With one, people talk about you for a day or a week or maybe a few months. With the other, people tell stories about you for the rest of your life and long after you're gone.

HERE'S A QUESTION: If you were in charge of writing a dictionary, how would you describe, in your own words, the difference between a champion and a legend?

HERE'S A CHALLENGE: Will you commit to being more than a champion and to becoming a legend in your world? I know, it might sound daunting and you may be thinking, *I could* never *be a legend!* But with God on your side, you can! (I'll give you some specific pointers on this later in the chapter.)

HERE'S SOME ENCOURAGEMENT: There is something legendary inside of you. God put it there Himself. The process of becoming a legend will mean facing some fears, but the more you walk with God and let the Holy Spirit lead your life, the more your legendaryness comes out.

HERE'S HOW YOU CAN PRAY: *Lord, fix my eyes on what is eternal. In every battle I find myself up against, help me to fight for Your victory, not my own. Thank You that I don't have to look like a champion to the world to leave a legacy for Your kingdom.*

TAKE NOTE: Some people who hear about that idea would immediately think, *Oh, yeah. That's me. I'm already a legend.* And others would really struggle with the idea of ever becoming more than they are right now. They're just hoping to graduate high school. I get it. But I also hope to inspire you to reach your fullest potential for greatness, which is *unlimited* with God. Would you take some time today to think about what you'd like your legacy to be? Write about it. Sing about it. Draw a picture of it. Capture it in a photo. However you want to express it is fine. Just begin to get your brain around it and create something you can look at to remind you of it.

A STORY THAT NEVER GETS OLD

Though I've heard the story of David and Goliath for as long as I can remember, I never get tired of it, and I often learn something new when I reread it. I hope you'll learn some new lessons from it as we focus on it in this chapter. You can find the whole story in 1 Samuel 17, but it starts when the Philistines (Goliath's people) and the Israelites (David's people) found themselves face-to-face against each other with a valley between them (1 Samuel 17:1–3). The Philistines' military hero, Goliath, wanted to fight the Israelites. First Samuel 17:4–7 describes him—in a fairly scary way!

> Then Goliath, a Philistine champion from Gath, came out of the Philistine ranks to face the forces of Israel. He was over nine feet tall! He wore a bronze helmet, and his bronze coat of mail weighed 125 pounds. He also wore bronze leg armor, and he carried a bronze javelin on his shoulder. The shaft of his spear was as heavy and thick as a weaver's beam, tipped with an iron spearhead that weighed 15 pounds. His armor bearer walked ahead of him carrying a shield.

Think about how big and strong Goliath had to be to wear armor that weighed 125 pounds, while also wearing a bronze helmet and bronze on his legs. Bronze is *heavy*! In addition, the tip of his spearhead weighed fifteen pounds. Next time you go to the gym for a workout, pick up a fifteen-pound weight and hold it while you extend your arm. It's not easy! Just like the guy in fifth-grade gym class, Goliath was the stud—the biggest of all with the best equipment for battle. His strengths outnumbered everyone else's.

As the Israelites stood looking at this giant covered in metal with his top-rate weapons, Goliath challenged them with a taunt:

> "Why are you all coming out to fight?" he called. "I am the Philistine champion, but you are only the servants of Saul. Choose one man to come down here and fight me! If he kills me, then we will be your slaves. But if I kill him, you will be our slaves!" (1 Samuel 17:8–9 NLT)

A lot was at stake in this battle. No wonder verse 11 says, "When Saul and the Israelites heard this, they were terrified and deeply shaken" (NLT).

About that time, David's father sent him to take food to his older brothers, who were with Saul and his soldiers. Young David heard Goliath taunt the Israelites again and began asking, "What will a man get for killing this Philistine and ending his defiance of Israel? Who is this pagan Philistine anyway, that he is allowed to defy the armies of the living God?" (v. 26 NLT). When Saul heard about David and his questions, he sent for him. David went to him and basically said, "Pick me! Put me in! I can do it!" This was his game changer, his chance to plant a seed of greatness in his life, and he knew it.

> **If anyone ever had a good reason to fear anything, it was David when he saw Goliath.**

But look at what happens in verse 33: "'Don't be ridiculous!' Saul replied. 'There's no way you can fight this Philistine and possibly win! You're only a boy, and he's been a man of war since his youth'" (NLT).

If anyone ever had a good reason to fear anything, it was David when he saw Goliath. He should have been shaking in his sandals in front of a fierce, metal-covered giant, but he wasn't. He is the poster child for living fearless! He stepped up to the challenge immediately, pushed back against what Saul was saying, and persisted. In 1 Samuel 17:34–37, he says:

> I have been taking care of my father's sheep and goats . . . When a lion or a bear comes to steal a lamb from the flock, I go after it with a club and rescue the lamb from its mouth. If the animal turns on me, I catch it by the jaw and club it to death. I have done this to both lions and bears, and I'll do it to this pagan Philistine, too, for he has defied the armies of the living God! The LORD who rescued me from the claws of the lion and the bear will rescue me from this Philistine! (NLT)

The end of verse 37 says, "Saul finally consented. 'All right, go ahead,' he said. 'And may the LORD be with you!'" (NLT).

We look at what God has given us. And we realize that what He has given us is enough, with His help and His grace, to find our way to victory in every battle.

The most beautiful part of the story to me is that David looks at his hands and sees hands that God made. He looks at his fingers and thinks about what they had accomplished in the past. He realizes what God has equipped him with. Then he hears an encouraging word from Saul, and off he goes to slay the giant.

Sometimes all it takes to win a battle is a game-changing opportunity and a "ten out of ten," meaning to give it all we've got, to be the very best we can be, holding nothing back. Sometimes all we need to gain victory in life is to be like David. We just look at what we have, what is before us, and we see the good in it. We don't think about what we can't do or what we don't have. We look at what God has given us. And we realize that what He has given us is enough, with His help and His grace, to find our way to victory in every battle. That's what it took for David. That's what it took for my friend Taylor (told you not to forget about him!). And that's where a valuable lesson is for you and me.

A LEGEND FINISHES WELL

This story ends in the most beautiful way—because that's what legends do. They make sure their stories end powerfully, appropriately, and in such a way that the story will live on after they are gone. First Samuel 17:51 tells us what ultimately happened to Goliath in very simple terms: "Then David ran over and pulled Goliath's sword from its sheath. David used it to kill him and cut off his head" (NLT).

All of this took place when David was young, so the story of his life and legacy went on for years. After he killed Goliath, David answered a question from Saul, and his answer gives us insight into his character. In verse 58, we read: "'Tell me about your father, young man,' Saul said. And David replied, 'His name is Jesse, and we live in Bethlehem'" (NLT).

Do you see that? David didn't just bask in all the glory of his heroic accomplishment, he didn't just answer with his father's name, but he told where he came from. Bethlehem was a humble town, not known for warriors or kings, and David demonstrated his humility by saying essentially, "Yep. That's where I come from. I am who I am. I know my God, and I just used what He gave me and moved forward in faith that He would protect me and win that battle."

I wonder, what if we did that daily? What if we woke up and realized every day what it means to be a ten out of ten with the hands we have been given? What if each day we used to the best of our ability what God has uniquely put inside of us to change the world? And what if at the end of each day we weren't interested in accolades or applause, but we extended our hands toward heaven and gave all the credit to the One who gave us our skills and talents? If we will do that, our lives will no longer be about what we can do, but about what God can do through the hands He made for us to use. That's what leaves a legacy.

HERE'S A QUESTION: What would it mean to you personally to be a ten out of ten?

HERE'S A CHALLENGE: When you see God, you can see the opportunities He puts in front of you—like David did. When you see God, you can see hope for your future. You can look beyond the battles of life, beyond all your opponents, and you can see what you have that can change the situation. Will you look for God—I mean, everywhere—today and for the rest of your life? That's my challenge. Just look for Him, and when you see Him, do what He wants you to do.

HERE'S SOME ENCOURAGEMENT: When you use what God has given you to do what He calls and equips you to do, it may mean boldly facing something that seems unbeatable, just as Goliath seemed undefeatable to everyone except David. You can choose to be like David, not like the crowd. Believe that God is with you, fighting for you, and leading you to the win!

HERE'S HOW YOU CAN PRAY: *Lord, enlighten my eyes to see Your side of victory and help me to walk with confidence that You are always on my side, fighting for me.*

FIVE WAYS LEGENDS DEFEAT FEAR

A champion is only a champion until the next person beats him or her, but a legend leaves a legacy that lasts a lifetime. So what are you going to be? A champion or a legend?

I hope and pray you want to be a legend, and I can tell you that the first step in that direction is to deal with fear. Here are five ways people who are legends overcome the things that make them anxious, intimidated, or fearful.

1. LEGENDS KNOW THAT GOD IS ON THEIR SIDE. David was an Israelite, and the Israelites knew they were God's covenant people. Their covenant connection

with Him was unbreakable. When people have an unbreakable connection, they fight together. They are on each other's side.

The sign of the Old Testament covenant was circumcision. When David referred to Goliath as "this uncircumcised Philistine," he was pointing out the fact that as an Israelite, he could depend on God to fight for him (1 Samuel 17:26 NKJV). As a Philistine, Goliath could not. David saw immediately that Goliath did not have the benefits of covenant relationship with God, and he knew he did. That's why he was so sure he would win the battle.

If you are in relationship with God through Jesus Christ, you too are in covenant with Him. That means He's on your side. And when God is on your side (meaning, you're on His), your victory is guaranteed.

2. LEGENDS DON'T LET THEMSELVES BE INTIMIDATED. If anyone ever had a right to be intimidated, it was David. Remember, Goliath was enormous. Many commentaries guess that he was probably about nine-and-a-half-feet tall. In addition, we know he was bulked up because he was strong enough to carry all that bronze!

But David walked in the fear of the Lord, not the fear of other people. He knew God was with him and did not want His people taunted or defeated. Regardless of what he saw with his natural eyes (a fierce giant), he kept his spiritual eyes focused on God. Maybe that's why he could write with such confidence: "With God we will gain the victory, and he will trample down our enemies" (Psalm 108:13).

You have no reason to be intimidated. Ever! The Enemy loves to use fear and intimidation to keep people from moving forward into what God has for them. There are plenty of intimidating people and situations in the world, I know. But you can choose to stare them down in the name of Jesus, knowing that He is with you and will let you triumph. After all, 2 Corinthians 2:14 says, "In Christ, God leads us from place to place in one perpetual victory parade" (MSG). Another translation says that in Jesus, God "always leads us in triumph" (NKJV).

3. LEGENDS REMEMBER WHO THEY ARE, WHO GOD IS, AND WHAT THEY HAVE ACCOMPLISHED. When David told Saul all he had done as a shepherd and how he had fought and defeated lions and bears, he was not only talking about his accomplishments; he was speaking out about his faith in God, the One who had always made him successful in a fight. Knowing that God had done this in the past gave David confidence that God could and would do it again. David knew he was not his own; he belonged to God. Convinced that God had given him strength and skill for battles, David knew that He would be with him again.

When you face life's battles, it's so important to remember who you are, what God has given you, who God is in your life, and what successes you have had in the past. Maybe you haven't killed lions and bears with your bare hands, but I'm pretty sure you can think of something good God has done for you and through you.

4. LEGENDS FIGHT WITH THEIR OWN ARMOR. When David offered to fight Goliath, Saul said it was a ridiculous idea. Of course, it wasn't. But what *was* ridiculous was the sight of David bumbling around in Saul's armor (see 1 Samuel 17:38). It didn't fit him, and he was not used to it.

When you find yourself up against a giant in your life, people may treat you like Saul treated David. They may want you to fight your battles with the equipment they use to fight their battles. That is, they may give you well-meaning advice that works for them, but it won't necessarily work for you. For example, I have a friend who is pretty laid-back and always tries to handle situations in a gentle, low-key way, keeping the peace as much as possible. She has a cousin who is extremely type-A. The two of them have a close relationship, but anytime my friend tells her cousin about a problem, the cousin urges her to handle it in a very strong, confrontational way and to get things stirred up. That's not my friend's nature. The same way David tried Saul's armor, she has tried it, and it hasn't been effective for her. Why? Because it doesn't flow from who she is. It flows from who someone else is.

When you find yourself needing to win a victory in some area of your life, it's so important to know who you are and to know what strategies and armor are right for you.

5. LEGENDS GIVE GOD THE GLORY. When David fought Goliath, he gave God the credit for his win before the battle even started. When he went out, slingshot in hand, to meet Goliath as the Israelites' chosen warrior, Goliath mocked him saying, "Am I a dog . . . that you come at me with a stick? . . . Come over here, and I'll give your flesh to the birds and wild animals!" (1 Samuel 17:43–44 NLT).

Notice David's bold response in verses 45–47:

> You come to me with sword, spear, and javelin, but I come to you in the name of the LORD of Heaven's Armies—the God of the armies of Israel, whom you have defied. Today the Lord will conquer you, and I will kill you and cut off your head. And then I will give the dead bodies of your men to birds and wild animals, and the whole world will know that there is a God in Israel! And everyone assembled here will know that the LORD rescues his people, but not with sword and spear. This is the LORD's battle, and he will give you to us! (NLT)

Legends don't take credit for their victories. They know their success rests on the fact that God has created them and given them their skills.

Before David loaded the stone into his slingshot, he was already sending the message to everyone around him that God would get the credit when he defeated Goliath. He basically said: "This is about God. Goliath has spoken against God, and that's not okay. I'm fighting in the name of God, which represents all that God is. God Himself will conquer you. I'm just going to slay you with this slingshot and then cut off your head. But this isn't about me. It's about God, and this is His battle to win."

Legends don't take credit for their victories. They know their success rests on the fact that God has created them and given them their skills. They recognize that He has put the right equipment in their hands, and that they have no reason to be intimidated because they are totally convinced that God has not given them "a spirit of fear, but of power and of love and of a sound mind" (2 Timothy

1:7 NKJV). Understanding that no matter how wonderful their accomplishments may seem, they couldn't pull them off alone, legends know that God is in every victory they win. And they happily give Him credit and thanks.

So-o-o . . .

* Remember my friend Taylor? All he needed in order to begin discovering what's legendary inside of him was a game-changing opportunity and a little time-out. He found that opportunity when he realized he could focus on what was good about himself instead of what he viewed as negative. David did the same thing. You too can choose to focus on what's positive about you.
* Legends can learn five lessons about overcoming fear from David: know that God is on your side; don't let yourself be intimidated; remember who you are, who God is, and what you have accomplished; fight with your own armor; and give God the glory.
* The first step toward becoming the legend God created you to be is to overcome your fears.

Work the Word

Praise the Lord, my soul.
Lord my God, you are very great;
    you are clothed with splendor and majesty.
The Lord wraps himself in light as with a garment;
    he stretches out the heavens like a tent
    and lays the beams of his upper chambers on their
        waters.
He makes the clouds his chariot
    and rides on the wings of the wind.

Psalm 104:1–3

I mentioned earlier in the book that I used to be *terrified* of tornadoes and other natural disasters. And not just when I was in kindergarten or elementary school. I mean until after I graduated high school. I was basically an adult still struggling with my childhood fears. (Yep, I could write a whole chapter on that, but I'm not going to go there right now).

One night a friend and I were staying in a guest room in a barn that belonged to another friend who lives near Nashville, Tennessee. I could not believe how ferocious the wind was that night! It was January, and the weather was already cold, but I wouldn't be surprised if the wind-chill factor that night made the temperature feel forty degrees colder. It was not an ordinary winter wind but one so strong I could hear it, and it actually frightened me.

At that time in my life, I was serious about my journey out of fear. I had learned not to completely freak out over the weather, but to pray or read God's Word. So I picked up my Bible, asked God to speak to me, and could hardly believe what I read. Yep, Psalm 104:1–3, which you just read. When I read that God "rides on the wings of the wind," everything began to change for me. Now I love the wind because it reminds me of God.

God is amazing. He took something that had caused me to be afraid for years, and in just a few minutes, He showed me that I didn't have to fear the wind at all. In fact, I could find strength and comfort in it. That's part of what's so powerful about God—He always finds a way to speak into your stuff.

He'd been speaking into my stuff for a long time through His Word, but I didn't know it because I didn't open the Book! The power of God's Word and the comfort of the Holy Spirit were there for me all the time; I just had to look for them.

Whether it's wind, water, clouds, or leaves on trees, when you see something in nature, look for God in it. Whenever you see something He created, you can find Him in it. And whenever you find Him, you can overcome your fears. Every time you take a step of faith, it's like knocking the breath out of fear.

8

Pick Your Partner

We learn by practice. Whether it means to learn to dance by practicing dancing or to learn to live by practicing living, the principles are the same.

Martha Graham

AS I MENTIONED AT THE BEGINNING OF THE book, a few years ago, I found myself on a journey that I never would have dreamed of going on. They asked me to dance. Not just any "they," but they who are in charge of *Dancing with the Stars.* That's a major "they."

I wrote in an earlier chapter about finding out they wanted me to participate in the show. Maybe you remember: I wanted to do it. Then I didn't want to do it. They didn't call, and I was sad. Then they did call to say they wanted me, and I had a meltdown about that. I got off to a dramatic start, and in this chapter, I want to share the rest of the story.

I remember the first night of the competition. I'd been thrown into a dance where I had to hang on to just about everything—my faith, my confidence, the fact that I had rehearsed the moves over and over, and especially my partner—just to get through it. Right before Mark and I took the floor, my head started spinning, my heart started beating, and my anxiety went off like an alarm. As I said, I had to hang on to all kinds of things just to finish the dance. When it was over, I hung on to my family and friends, favorable remarks from the judges, the comments people made about the performance, and the articles and reviews I read. Why wouldn't I have done that? Everything was so positive! The reviews and comments were amazing. They lasted exactly one week.

All of a sudden, I went from fabulous to mediocre. And that quick turn of events taught me one of the most valuable lessons of my life—that applause and public affirmation could never sustain me.

When week two rolled around, I found myself in the middle of a different story. I still had a great partner and the never-ending support of my family and friends, but the judges and the general public weren't nearly as impressed with the second dance as they were with the first one. All of a sudden, I went from fabulous to mediocre. And that quick turn of events taught me one of the most valuable lessons of my life—that applause and public affirmation could never sustain me. I could not let what other people thought or said about me affect what I thought and said about myself. I learned three words that stung at first, but then drove me to a place of faith in God I had never known before: *people are fickle* (that's one reason the fear of others is never good).

People change. Their comments and opinions change. One day they can think you are the most awesome person on earth, but the next day they think you're a worm—and someone else is the greatest on earth. My experience during the first two weeks of *Dancing with the Stars* was my introduction to that truth, but now that I've learned it, it's been a fact of life for me for quite a while.

HERE'S A QUESTION: Have you ever depended too much on what other people think or say about you? (That's called the fear of man.)

HERE'S A CHALLENGE: It's time to stop relying on other people for your sense of value and to stop letting their opinions determine what you think about yourself. I challenge you to do that.

HERE'S SOME ENCOURAGEMENT: Yep. People are fickle. There's only one person who has ever lived who does not change. *Ever.* I can't say it any better than this: "Jesus Christ is the same yesterday and today and forever" (Hebrews 13:8). If you want someone in your life you can always depend on, He's the One.

HERE'S HOW YOU CAN PRAY: *Abba Father, today I want to focus on who You say I am. I go back to every word the world has said I am and I cover it with who You say I am. Thank You for always being a Father and for supporting me as a daughter [or son] yesterday, today, and forever. I rejoice in knowing that You take delight in me.*

(Note: Scripture uses many names to describe God. "Abba Father" is one of the most significant because of how it relates to us. Translated from the Aramaic language, it means "Daddy.")

TAKE NOTE: When people let you down, it's a terrible feeling. Maybe you've been there. Now would be a good time to journal about how you felt when you discovered that people are fickle and what you've learned since then.

If you read Luke 4 (and I suggest you take time to do that right now), you'll see that when Jesus announced in the synagogue that He was the One the prophet Isaiah had prophesied, everyone went crazy with excitement—at first (Luke 4:22). Six verses later, they all hated Him and wanted Him dead. *Six verses!* That's how I know He totally understands when you and I feel like everyone loves us for a while and then suddenly they can't find anything good to say about us.

For me this turnaround took one week. During week one of the show, they loved me. I was second on the leader board. All the articles were awesome, but then the next week the articles were controversial and I was in jeopardy. That shook me. And the fact that it shook me, . . . shook me. It was a challenge to my identity and to my faith—a challenge unlike any I had faced before. I had to decide how to handle it. I could fall into the old fear-of-other-people trap—being afraid they wouldn't like my dance, afraid they would think I was awkward, afraid they would criticize my outfit, afraid I'd embarrass myself, and on and on. Or I could take authority over fear in Jesus' name and keep going. To help make that decision, I asked myself three very important questions:

1. WHOSE VOICE IS THE LOUDEST IN MY LIFE? Was it mine, the judges, the audience's, my family's, my partner's? Was it my fears and anxieties? Or was it God's? There were so many voices saying so many different things that I had to decide to mute some of them, turn down others, and put God's on full blast.

2. WHOSE LEAD IS THE STRONGEST IN MY LIFE? I had lots of options when it came to whose lead I wanted to follow—all the same people whose voices I heard. Was I going to follow one of them or follow God?

3. WHAT'S MY IDEA OF WINNING? Most people who watched the show thought winning meant coming in in first place, having higher scores than everyone else, and being declared the winner. As I thought about it, I realized that I didn't need any of those things to win. If I knew who I was in God and who He was in me, I won. I'm going to say more about my idea of winning in the next section of this chapter, but for now let me simply say that the Bible is clear about it: "Thanks be to God! He gives us the victory through our Lord Jesus Christ" (1 Corinthians 15:57).

TAKE NOTE: The three questions I asked myself were huge. They were incredibly important in the development of my identity and my faith. So let me ask you the three questions I asked myself: Whose voice is loudest in your life? Whose lead is strongest in your life? And what is your idea of winning?

EVERYBODY'S ON A PATH

I hope you've taken time to really think about your idea of winning. It may not be what anyone else around you considers a victory, but if you can settle in your heart what winning means for you and God, then you've gained a big victory already.

I've always felt that when people watch *Dancing with the Stars,* they can tell which performers are on which paths. That is, every season, some people will do whatever it takes to get the mirror-ball trophy. That's their goal, and that's what winning means to them. Then there are other people who are happy simply to be on the show, and they love the journey.

One person who loved the journey is my good friend Michael Waltrip. I think the fact that he so thoroughly enjoyed being on the show is what endeared him to millions of people. He made it so far because he knew who he was and he embraced it and shared it with the world. Was he the best dancer? Not so much. But he has one of the biggest hearts of anyone I've ever known, and that brought joy into homes across America and around the world. People loved him!

Enjoying the journey helps people like Michael to experience a measure of success on the show, while it causes others, who may be excellent dancers, to go home early in the season. Their skills and techniques may be nearly perfect, but if for them that trumps having fun and being grateful for the opportunity to be on the show, the audience can tell. Something's missing. When people are fiercely determined to get more points than everyone else and come in first, and that's their idea of winning, it's easy for them to lose sight of who they really are and to pass up finding joy in other aspects of the experience.

It's the heart, the journey, and the ability to share them that matter. Anything else is just a competition, and competitions can be very sad and empty.

Now don't get me wrong. There are also some rare breeds like Alfonso. He wanted the mirror ball with a passion. He pursued it while also staying true to himself, and that's why he deserved to be champion.

I learned through my experience on *Dancing with the Stars* that people don't just want to see breathtaking, dramatic dance moves. They want to witness and relate to the journeys the performers are on as human beings. When hearts connect on that kind of level, it goes beyond a show on which people learn to dance. This is true for any life situation, not only *Dancing with the Stars.* It's the heart, the journey, and the ability to share them that matter. Anything else is just a competition, and competitions can be very sad and empty. I'm sure you have noticed that fact in high school, in college, or in the workplace. Maybe you've even felt it for yourself. You see, when people lose their identity in order to get to the top, they begin to lose everything. I'll explain this using the example of the two-step.

To kids today, the two-step is a rap dance spun off of a popular rap song. To other people, especially those beyond their teenage years, it's an old country dance. I once told Two-Mama that I knew how to do the two-step and she said, "We used to do that back in my day!" Of course, I was shocked because the two-step I was talking about seemed to be a weird dance for a grandma to do. I started doing today's version of the two-step for her, and she quickly realized it was *not* the two-step she learned. The world had changed since she did the dance and it became something it was never intended to be. It just had the same name.

When we let times or circumstances change us, we often don't realize the problem it causes.

Something similar often happens to us. Like the two-step, we keep the same names but stray far away from our original selves because times change and we do not realize we are changing with them (kind of like that time I lost my peace and didn't even know it). When we let times or circumstances change us, we often don't realize the problem it causes. Our steps get a little ahead of us and we just follow where the world goes. We end up with a dance no one even recognizes anymore; we ourselves don't even know what it is. We say, "I'm the same person," but we have truly moved far away from our original selves.

We live in a competitive world, and perhaps the only competition truly worth winning is the one we have with ourselves—the battle to be true to ourselves and to maintain our identity when the world tries to get us to go after its trophies.

HERE'S A QUESTION: Can you think of a time when you lost your identity as you tried to win in life? If so, how did that happen?

HERE'S A CHALLENGE: Your identity is one of the most foundational pieces of your life. I challenge you to discover, or rediscover, who you really are.

HERE'S SOME ENCOURAGEMENT: It's never too late to figure out who you are or to change course as you try to win in life. God's always eager to use His eraser on your past and give you a fresh start.

HERE'S HOW YOU CAN PRAY: *Father, I'm sorry that I've drifted so far from my original self in search of things that will not sustain me. I realize now that my confidence, my freedom, and my faith come only in You. You are the One I'm running after. Lead me from this world of darkness into Your heavenly light.*

TAKE NOTE: It's important to me to ask this question, and it's even more important for you to answer it: Who are you? I'm not talking about what you like to do in your free time or what you like to read about or listen to. I mean, who are you—really, at your core?

DO YOU WANT TO DANCE?

When I started on *Dancing with the Stars*, not only did I not know how to dance, but I didn't understand my identity. I had no direction, and I felt lost at first, but quickly I found myself learning to dance with Jesus—finding out who He made me to be and who I was in Him, not in myself. To do that, though, I had to get rid of all the unhealthy things I was holding on to. For example, I got someone else to run my Twitter account, and I never read comments online or in the media. In addition, Mark translated what the judges said in a constructive, healthy way, and I decided that to me, winning was not the mirror-ball trophy. Winning would be conquering fear and learning how to find who I am through the words God speaks about who I am.

A lot of you watched me on this journey of learning to dance with Jesus while actually learning to dance. It was a crazy ride. I think sometimes we have to take a step back and identify our ultimate goal. Choosing not to go hard after the mirror ball helped me in my decision making about a lot of things, because it really didn't matter if I "won" or not. It helped my perspective to be pure instead of smeared by the world. That's what made it easy to say no to "cool moves" that did not represent me well and to say no to super-cute outfits that showed just a little too much for my personal taste. This perspective taught me to not only make the right decisions because I had to, but to live those right decisions with a happy heart because I wanted to respect my ultimate partner, Jesus.

Dance is a respectful sport. That's why I chose never to say in an interview that I wanted to win or asked people to *please* vote for me. (This made Mark really mad. He didn't really understand my approach, but once he saw the joy in my heart after Alfonso won, he got it. Mark is like a brother to me, and brothers just want the best for their sisters). The Lord wanted me to fully fall in step with Him and find victory in that.

I think sometimes we have to take a step back and identify our ultimate goal.

During my time on

Dancing with the Stars, God carried me through every step, every interview, and every conversation, and I began learning how to follow confidently. After all, dance is about confidence, going into every move with full confidence that the next move will be amazing. Whether it's the right move or the wrong move, confidence can sell it.

To be confident in your dancing, you have to be confident in your partner, trusting that he will lead you where he is going. When I watched *Dancing with the Stars* growing up, I always thought it was so much easier for the guys because it looked like a lot of times the girls could cover them by dancing around them. Being there, I realized it's actually easier for the girls to learn to make a beautiful dance together, as long as they have a good partner, because the male is the leader. Many times Mark would give my hand a little push or pull to make sure I was back to the original dance and on track for the next move. He could do this because the dance was his masterpiece, which he created. He knew it better than anyone, and more than anyone, he wanted it to be the best it could be. So I learned how to follow that push or pull. I trusted that he knew how to lead me because, as I said, he created the dance.

It's just like your life. God is the one who created you. He wrote your story. He also extends His words and His love to lead you, and He will not lead you where He is not going. When you dance down your path of life with Him, He may tug you or pull you in one direction, and it's *vital* to fully embrace that next move confidently, knowing He is pushing you into the step He has created for you. It's important to take note that you will also have judges in your life. You may have scores. You may be put in "competition," but it's up to you to find out who you really are and to decide whose voice is louder, whose lead is stronger, and what winning ultimately means to you.

So-o-o . . .

* People are fickle. They will love you some days, but not so much on other days. The only constant in this world is Jesus.
* The race to be "the best" or to come away from a competition with a prize or the highest number of points isn't what's most important. What matters most is that you discover who you really are and live your life from your true identity, fearing nothing.
* God created you and He knows exactly how to lead you in the dance of your life. All you have to do is pay attention to the nudges and follow Him.

Work the Word

"In your anger do not sin": Do not let the sun go down while you are still angry.

Ephesians 4:26

I don't have many memories of my great-grandfather, but I still have a lot of love for him. He was a great guy! One memory that stands out to me clearly is that when I was very young, he walked into the room where I was playing one day and said, "Remember this. It's the greatest piece of advice anyone has ever given me." And then he quoted Ephesians 4:26.

People might say, "Well, I can't just push a button and turn off my anger because the sun goes down! It's not that easy!" I think what my grandfather was saying, and perhaps what this verse is trying to communicate, is that when we become angry over something, we need to move quickly to establish peace in our hearts.

This verse is as true for fear as it is for anger. When we become really fearful about something, we need to get back to a place of peace as fast as we can. That doesn't mean a battle with fear will be over by the time night rolls around, but we can change the posture of our hearts. We don't have to hold on to the fear. We can choose peace, joy, strength, courage, and faith in the midst of it.

God never says everything in life will be wonderful. He doesn't promise we won't face things that are frightening. But He does promise to be with us in the scary situations. He does promise to give us peace. And He does promise He will never leave us.

When we allow anger or fear to upset us and we forget these promises, let's bring these realities back to the forefront of our minds as fast as we can and keep our hearts focused on them.

One More Thing

A Word That Changes Everything

At the cross God wrapped His heart
in flesh and blood and let it be nailed
to the cross for our redemption.

E. Stanley Jones

DO YOU REMEMBER THE CHAPTER ABOUT plankton? I mentioned there that plankton are wanderers and that the root of their name even means "wandering." When I was learning about plankton, the thought occurred to me that there are lots of wanderings and wanderers in the Bible. And these wanderings usually weren't good experiences. Think about it. In the

Old Testament, the Israelites spent forty years wandering around in the wilderness to make what should have been an eleven-day journey. In the New Testament, the prodigal son went wandering all over the place, walking on the wild side wherever he went, before he finally came to his senses and returned to his father's house.

I think we all have a little bit of a wanderer in us. Don't we all get off the path of life at times?

I think we all have a little bit of a wanderer in us. Don't we all get off the path of life at times? Don't we all let our hearts and minds stray from God and from His Word on occasion? Sure we do—and when we do, what matters most isn't that we've wandered, but that we get back to God.

Ideally, we would live our lives so in love with God that when we wander, we would always end up back in His presence. We would hunger so much for Him that our wanderings would take us closer to Him, not further from Him. But it doesn't always work that way. Sometimes we wander, like my friend Taylor, and we keep on running from God until He sends someone or something to stop us and help us find our way back to Him.

I want to encourage you today, if you have wandered away from God, get back to Him. Pull out your Bible and start reading it again. Begin to talk to God in prayer again, and be looking for His answers. Reconnect with your Christian friends. Find an adult who loves and walks with God who is willing to mentor you and help you grow stronger in your faith. Go back to church, where you can learn about God and worship Him. Why not start right now by simply praying something like this: *God I've wandered away from You, but I am ready to come home. I'm sorry for the ways I've turned my back on You. I ask You to forgive me. I believe You forgive me, and I receive Your forgiveness. Help me make a fresh start with You. I choose today to be devoted to You, sold out in my faith, and diligent to know and live by Your Word.*

The Holy Spirit will always draw us toward God. And as we allow ourselves to be led into God's presence, just imagine the light we can receive and then share with others. I pray you will be like plankton and go vertical with your life, which will turn your restless wandering into great purpose.

WHAT'S THE WORD?

The title of this section is, "A Word that Changes Everything," so you're probably wondering what that word might be. There are lots of words that change everything, but the one I'm thinking of is *redemption.* When I Googled it, two definitions came up: (1) "The action of saving or being saved from sin, error, or evil." (2) "The action of regaining or gaining possession of something in exchange for payment, or clearing a debt."[1] So whether you've wandered from God or you have never been in a relationship with Him and you'd like to be, *redemption* is a word that can change everything in your life.

If you've wandered, it means God will gladly take you back. If you've never had a personal relationship with Him, it means you're invited and welcome to do that right now by praying this prayer aloud:

Father,

You love me so much that You chose to see the beauty of my broken soul. You love me so much that You sent Your Son to freely forgive me for the path of pain, fear, bitterness, and many other things I have walked through. But Your Word says we are saved by grace through faith—faith we have in the beautiful gift of Your Son. I believe and I confess with my mouth that You are who You say You are, that You will do what you say You will do through Your Son, Jesus Christ, who died on the cross and rose three days later to bring me hope, freedom, love, salvation, and redemption. I believe that He is alive today! I am sorry for my sins, and I ask You to forgive me, Father. By faith I receive Jesus Christ as my Lord and Savior. I am so grateful to be fully known and loved by You. In the name of Jesus, amen.

I didn't write this book simply to share the story of my own redemption and my journey out of the fear that once consumed me. I wrote it to help you find *your* redemption. I encourage you not to do this in your room alone, but to find a trustworthy pastor or Christian friend who can help you take the next steps of your walk of faith—baptism, learning more about God, prayer, and ongoing, life-changing relationship with Jesus through the Word of God.

Like the woman who was caught in adultery and then had an encounter with Jesus and heard Him say, "Go and sin no more," that's His ideal for all of us (John 8:11 NKJV). But we do sin, so where does that leave us? In a place where we sin less and less because we honor and value the grace that's been given to us, because we know it is a precious gift that cost Him His life, and because we would never want to take advantage of the gift of grace.

Find a trustworthy pastor or Christian friend who can help you take the next steps of your walk of faith.

A MAN WHO REFUSED REDEMPTION

I was on my way to a speaking engagement—and running late because I forgot to account for the time change between where I live in Franklin, Tennessee, and where I was speaking in Atlanta, Georgia. My team and I were hurrying to the venue, about seven minutes away, when something amazing happened.

First let me back up and say that the entire day, I had wrestled with an unusual feeling—a soberness and sense of responsibility I had not felt before. I sensed that God had entrusted me with a message through which He wanted to convey to the audience the heaviness, the greatness, the weight, and the power of His love. I knew He wanted me to go there, but I kept asking, "How do I get there?"

As we sat in traffic, I listened to a message from Priscilla Shirer, and one sentence caught my attention. She said, "God won't put His promises in your way, but He will put them within your reach."

No sooner than I heard those words, I looked out the car window and saw a homeless man. Across the intersection, he and I locked eyes. I prayed and asked God to send someone to help him. Aimlessly, the man walked up and down the sidewalk. I couldn't take my eyes off of him. As I watched, I heard in my heart some instructions from the Holy Spirit: "Go put it in his reach, and you'll know how I feel."

I knew what God wanted me to do. He wanted me to give the man my Bible. But we were already almost late for the meeting and I was one of the main speakers. I couldn't just not show up on time. At the same time, I couldn't disobey what I heard. It's like it was burning inside me. I couldn't even sit still. I told the person driving, "We *have* to turn around." I could not let that man go without talking to him.

"God won't put His promises in your way, but He will put them within your reach."

I had no money that night. All I had was my phone, my Bible, my speaking notes, and a few things in my purse that would not have been interesting or helpful to him. Yet I wanted more than anything else in the world to help this man. I felt compelled to do something for him—like I would burst if I didn't try.

The driver turned around and I got out of the car to approach the man, who was dirty and smelly and had an empty, hopeless look in his eyes.

"I honestly don't have anything to give you, but this Book is everything," I said as I held out the Bible to him.

"No! I can't take that," he responded.

"Sure you can," I said. "I *really* want to give it to you."

"No," he emphasized, then added, "I'm an atheist."

As I started to walk away, I noticed his eyes filling with tears. So I put the Bible on the ground, giving him a chance to pick it up.

"No!" he shouted as I headed back to the car. "Somebody needs that! Don't leave it on the ground!"

In that instant, my faith changed. In fact, my life changed. I realized how God must feel when people won't listen to Him, live by His Word, or receive His love. When I begged him to take it and he wouldn't, I could almost physically feel my heart break.

In the same moment, I realized how much the Word of God means to me and how deeply I believe it. No one would literally beg another person to take something useless, powerless, or meaningless. As I begged the man to take it,

In that instant, my faith changed. In fact, my life changed. I realized how God must feel when people won't listen to Him, live by His Word, or receive His love.

I realized how completely I am convinced that God's Word is where we find everything—everything—we need in life.

God is constantly reaching out to us through His Word, saying, "Here's life. Here's hope. Here's love.'" And so often we fail to take those things He so freely offers us.

As I thought about the encounter with the homeless man and reflected on how much that experience changed me, I thought, *He can say he's an atheist all day long, but he isn't.* How do I know that? By his words. When he said about the Bible, "Somebody needs that," he proved that he knew something about the life-changing power of God's Word, and I believe he saw the conviction of that truth in my eyes.

I beg you not to be like this man. In an instant, he could have gone from being spiritually homeless to having a forever home with God. He could have gone from being fatherless to having the best Father ever. He could have gone from lying on the ground to standing tall in faith. But he chose not to (as far as I know).

God is extending redemption to you, just as He extended it to the homeless man. Whether you receive it for the first time or you use it to come back to God, do everything you can do to stay close to Him. Jesus says in John 15:16, "You did not choose me, but I chose you." That's amazing news! He's already chosen you, so all you have to do is keep choosing Him. If you want to hear more about this, check out my video "A Message to My Fellow College Age Friends" on my YouTube channel.

NO SHAME, NO REGRETS

Just a final thought before we finish this book. Often when people break free from fear, the Enemy then tries to make them feel ashamed or upset about the ways they once allowed fear to control them. I've been through that, and so have lots of other people. We used to let fear keep us from doing something fun, and letting it stop us seemed perfectly reasonable at the time. But once we came out from under fear's control, we could have done that thing and enjoyed it. In fact, we should have done it. We didn't escape something frightening; we missed out on a lot of fun.

Sometimes after the chains of fear are finally loosed, we realize how silly fear is and we become angry that we were ever afraid of anything. We're upset with ourselves and mad at fear for controlling us. We find ourselves filled with regret over our fear-based decisions.

These are real struggles, but we have to be aware that redemption affects our emotions; it sets us free from shame, anger, and regret. When we embrace the redemption Jesus offers us, we can say, "Okay, Lord. I'm sorry I let fear run my life for so long. I'm sorry I missed out on some great opportunities that came my way. But I believe that guilt, shame, anger, regret, and every other negative emotion and lie of the Enemy were dealt with at the cross. You died to set me free—not just from sin and death, but also from feelings of condemnation."

Don't let shame or regret steal your future the way fear has stolen your past. Receive the freedom Jesus died to give you, and move forward in faith to live the amazing life He has for you, never looking back.

Do Not Fear

Verses to Help You Live *Fearless*

"So do not fear, for I am with you;
do not be dismayed, for I am your God.
I will strengthen you and help you;
I will uphold you with my righteous right hand."

ISAIAH 41:10

Immediately [Jesus] spoke to them and said, "Take courage! It is I. Don't be afraid."

MARK 6:50

I sought the LORD, and he answered me;
he delivered me from all my fears.

PSALM 34:4

When I am afraid, I put my trust in you.

PSALM 56:3

Do not be anxious about anything, but in every situation, by prayer and petition, with thanksgiving, present your requests to God. And the peace of God, which transcends all understanding, will guard your hearts and your minds in Christ Jesus.

PHILIPPIANS 4:6–7

"Peace I leave with you; my peace I give you. I do not give to you as the world gives. Do not let your hearts be troubled and do not be afraid."

JOHN 14:27

There is no fear in love. But perfect love drives out fear, because fear has to do with punishment. The one who fears is not made perfect in love.

1 JOHN 4:18

When anxiety was great within me,
your consolation brought me joy.

PSALM 94:19

"Do not fear, for I have redeemed you;
I have summoned you by name; you are mine."

ISAIAH 43:1

The Lord is my light and my salvation—
whom shall I fear?
The Lord is the stronghold of my life—
of whom shall I be afraid?

PSALM 27:1

For the Spirit God gave us does not make us timid, but gives us power, love and self-discipline.

2 TIMOTHY 1:7

Anxiety weighs down the heart,
but a kind word cheers it up.

PROVERBS 12:25

Even though I walk
through the darkest valley,
I will fear no evil,
for you are with me;
your rod and your staff,
they comfort me.

PSALM 23:4

"Therefore do not worry about tomorrow, for tomorrow will worry about itself. Each day has enough trouble of its own."

MATTHEW 6:34

Humble yourselves, therefore, under God's mighty hand, that he may lift you up in due time. Cast all your anxiety on him because he cares for you.

1 PETER 5:6–7

Say to those with fearful hearts,
"Be strong, do not fear;
your God will come,
he will come with vengeance;
with divine retribution
he will come to save you."

ISAIAH 35:4

"Have I not commanded you? Be strong and courageous. Do not be afraid; do not be discouraged, for the LORD your God will be with you wherever you go."

JOSHUA 1:9

Cast your cares on the LORD
and he will sustain you;
he will never let
the righteous be shaken.

PSALM 55:22

“Do not worry about your life, what you will eat; or about your body, what you will wear. For life is more than food, and the body more than clothes. Consider the ravens: They do not sow or reap, they have no storeroom or barn; yet God feeds them. And how much more valuable you are than birds! Who of you by worrying can add a single hour to your life? Since you cannot do this very little thing, why do you worry about the rest?”

LUKE 12:22–26

Be strong and courageous. Do not be afraid or terrified because of them, for the LORD your God goes with you; he will never leave you nor forsake you.

DEUTERONOMY 31:6

“For I am the LORD your God
    who takes hold of your right hand
and says to you, Do not fear;
    I will help you.
Do not be afraid, you worm Jacob,
    little Israel, do not fear,
for I myself will help you,” declares the LORD,
    your Redeemer, the Holy One of Israel.

ISAIAH 41:13–14

God is our refuge and strength,
an ever-present help in trouble.

PSALM 46:1

Fear of man will prove to be a snare,
but whoever trusts in the LORD is kept safe.

PROVERBS 29:25

The LORD is with me; I will not be afraid.
What can mere mortals do to me?
The LORD is with me; he is my helper.
I look in triumph on my enemies.

PSALM 118:6–7

He got up, rebuked the wind and said to the waves, "Quiet! Be still!" Then the wind died down and it was completely calm.

He said to his disciples, "Why are you so afraid? Do you still have no faith?"

MARK 4:39–40

Even if you should suffer for what is right, you are blessed. "Do not fear their threats; do not be frightened."

1 PETER 3:14

Do not be afraid of them; the LORD your God himself will fight for you.

DEUTERONOMY 3:22

The angel of the Lord encamps around those who
fear him,
and he delivers them.

PSALM 34:7

He placed his right hand on me and said: "Do not be afraid. I am the First and the Last."

REVELATION 1:17

Jesus told him, "Don't be afraid; just believe."

MARK 5:36

For I am convinced that neither death nor life, neither angels nor demons, neither the present nor the future, nor any powers, neither height nor depth, nor anything else in all creation, will be able to separate us from the love of God that is in Christ Jesus our Lord.

ROMANS 8:38–39

The Lord your God is with you,
the Mighty Warrior who saves.
He will take great delight in you;
in his love he will no longer rebuke you,
but will rejoice over you with singing.

ZEPHANIAH 3:17

Whoever dwells in the shelter of the Most High
will rest in the shadow of the Almighty.
I will say of the Lord, "He is my refuge and my
fortress,
my God, in whom I trust."
Surely he will save you. . . .
He will cover you with his feathers,
and under his wings you will find refuge;
his faithfulness will be your shield and rampart.
You will not fear the terror of night,
nor the arrow that flies by day,
nor the pestilence that stalks in the darkness,
nor the plague that destroys at midday.

PSALM 91:1-6

Notes

Chapter 1: It's Not That Things Aren't Scary . . .

1. John Piper, "God is Most Glorified in Us When We Are Most Satisfied in Him," *Desiring God* (blog), October 13, 2012, http://www.desiringgod.org/messages/god-is-most-glorified-in-us-when-we-are-most-satisfied-in-him.

Chapter 2: Who, Me? Fearless?

1. "Facts and Statistics," Anxiety and Depression Association of America (website), https://adaa.org/about-adaa/press-room/facts-statistics.

Chapter 3: The Purpose of Plankton

1. *Wikipedia*, s.v. "plankton," accessed September 11, 2017, https://en.wikipedia.org/wiki/Plankton.
2. "Photosynthesis for Kids," Photosynthesis Education, accessed September 11, 2017, http://photosynthesiseducation.com/photosynthesis-for-kids/, italics added.
3. Amy Hansen, "Invisible Watery World," ASU School of Life Sciences, https://askabiologist.asu.edu/explore/plankton.

4. Dan Groody, quoted in West, “The Biblical Story as a Migration Story,” Kino Border Initiative, November 28, 2012, https://www.kinoborderinitiative.org/the-biblical-story-as-a-migration-story/.
5. Tim Elmore, “6 Fears and Concerns of College Students Today,” Growing Leaders, May 31, 2012, http://growingleaders.com/blog/6-fears-and-concerns-of-college-students-today.

Chapter 4: Jump Off the Crazy Train

1. John Piper, “You Are God’s Midwife for the New Birth of Others,” Desiring God (blog), April 6, 2008, http://www.desiringgod.org/messages/you-are-gods-midwife-for-the-new-birth-of-others.
2. Sadie Robertson Huff, "#CrazyTrain," YouTube, July 7, 2016, https://www.youtube.com/watch?v=hG16AhHlkjI.

Chapter 5: Connect the Dots

1. Eric Hoffer, *The Passionate State of Mind* (New York: Harper, 1955), 131.

One More Thing

1. Oxford Living Dictionaries, November 10, 2017, https://en.oxforddictionaries.com/definition/redemption.

Acknowledgments

THANK YOU TO MY DAD, WHO ALWAYS CHALlenges me and protects me.

Thank you to my siblings, who take me away from all the world's problems with the laughter we share. I cannot imagine my life without y'all.

Thank you to my best friends in the whole world, "the 3-mile stretch." The Lord outdid Himself when He put y'all in my life. I love doing life together. I cannot wait to blog now that this book is written.

Thank you to Mel, Margaret, and my Two-Papa for handling the business aspects of my publishing relationships and making it possible to have a book.

Thank you to Beth Clark for dreaming, creating, and praying with me on this journey of leading people to their redemption story. You put my heart on paper beautifully.

Our family loves you and wishes you the best on every single book you write. Your prayers are transparent on paper.

To my team—Courtney, Stephanie, and Juli. You all make these things happen. Thank you for being Spirit-led and for working so hard to pump content for this generation.

About the Author

Sadie Robertson Huff is a *New York Times* bestselling author, speaker, influencer, and founder of Live Original. Communicating as a sister and friend, Huff is on a mission to use her influence to reach her generation with the message of Christ. Huff is the host of the popular podcast *WHOA, That's Good,* which reached more than a million unique downloads after only fifteen episodes. Her *Live Original* blog features encouraging and transparent messages from Huff and her closest friends. She recently launched her exclusive online community and app, LO Sister, which is designed to cultivate sisterhood through Bible studies and workshops. You can learn more about Sadie Robertson Huff at LiveOrginal.com or by following her on Instagram @legitsadierob.

Praise for **LIVE** *Fearless*

"I can't think of a better role model for young girls than Sadie. The time I spent with Sadie and her family created some beautiful memories for me, and I am proud to call her family. Her positivity, generosity, and love for everyone around her is something rare these days. I hope one day my daughters look up to someone like Sadie. Congrats on the new book. Its message is something we all need right now."

—Mark Ballas, Emmy-nominated performer and singer-songwriter

"Sadie Robertson is a calming and powerful voice in a world that tries to keep us fearful and quiet. This book is a beautiful representation of not only what Sadie believes but also how she lives. It will grow you and change you, and you will not be the same after reading it."

—Annie F. Downs, bestselling author of *100 Days to Brave* and *Looking for Lovely*

"Sadie and her story continue to inspire so many around the world, including me. Both young people and adults can learn to live fearlessly through this incredible new book!"

—Nastia Liukin, five-time Olympic medalist

"Sadie is once in a generation. We can think of no better person to write about living fearless than someone who has already lived with such courage, bravery, and inspiration. We know this book will change your life if you let it."

—Jefferson and Alyssa Bethke,
authors of *Love That Lasts*

"Sadie Robertson is the walking example of what it means to allow God's glorious light to shine through us. In *Live Fearless,* Sadie uses her testimony along with the Word as tools to walk confidently in His grace and peace! Sadie is EXACTLY the voice and warrior this generation needs!"

—Alexa PenaVega, actress and singer

"*Live Fearless* could not be coming out at a better time than right now. Fear is a paralyzing spirit that has such a stronghold in this generation. Sadie's honest and brave account of facing her own fears and overcoming them with courage and faith is inspiring and is a great testament that we can all overcome when we realize who lives inside of us. Sadie is a powerful young woman with a message of hope and transformation, and I'm so excited for you to read this message, get free of fear, and live according to how God made you to live."

—Alex Seeley, lead pastor of The Belonging Co.
Nashville and author of *Tailor Made*

LIVE *Fearless*

LIVE *Fearless*

LIVE *Fearless*

Live Fearless

Tommy Nelson, PO Box 141000, Nashville, TN 37214

Published in Nashville, Tennessee, by Tommy Nelson. Tommy Nelson is an imprint of Thomas Nelson. Thomas Nelson is a registered trademark of HarperCollins Christian Publishing, Inc.

Published in association with William Morris Endeavor Entertainment, LLC, c/o Mel Berger and Margaret Riley King, 11 Madison Avenue, New York, New York 10010.

Tommy Nelson titles may be purchased in bulk for educational, business, fund-raising, or sales promotional use. For information, please email SpecialMarkets@ThomasNelson.com.

ISBN 978-1-4002-0917-0 (audiobook)
ISBN 978-1-4003-0942-9 (eBook)
ISBN 978-1-4002-5589-4 (Deluxe hardcover)

The Library of Congress has cataloged the original edition as follows:

Names: Robertson, Sadie, 1997- author.
Title: Live fearless : a call to power, passion, and purpose / Sadie Robertson.
Description: Nashville : Thomas Nelson, 2018. | Includes bibliographical references. |
Identifiers: LCCN 2017055035 (print) | LCCN 2017056752 (ebook) | ISBN 9781400309429 (e-book) | ISBN 9781400309399 (hardcover)
Subjects: LCSH: Christian life. | Fear--Religious aspects--Christianity. | Teenage girls--Religious life. | Christian teenagers--Religious life.
Classification: LCC BV4509.5 (ebook) | LCC BV4509.5 .R626 2018 (print) | DDC 248.8/33--dc23
LC record available at https://lccn.loc.gov/2017055035

Cover design by Kathy Mitchell
Floral art on endpapers used by license: Adobe Stock/Good Studio.

Printed in India

25 26 27 28 29 MAI 10 9 8 7 6 5 4 3 2 1
Mfr: MAI / Manipal, India / September 2025 / PO #12319666